PASSING ON THE COMFORT

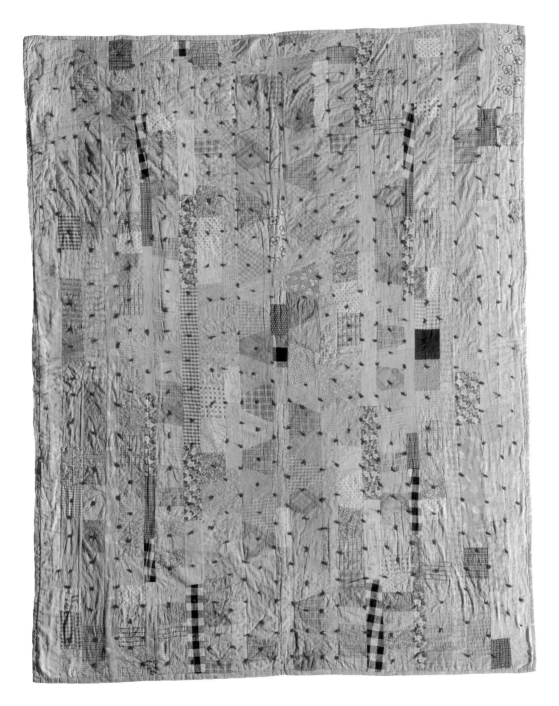

Bars and Tumblers Comforter, Number 1

PASSING ON THE COMFORT

*The War, The Quilts,
and the Women
Who Made a Difference*

An Keuning-Tichelaar
and Lynn Kaplanian-Buller

Good Books

Intercourse, PA 17534
800/762-7171
www.goodbks.com

Photographs by Donna Halvorsen (cover, page 174), by Merle Good (pages 2, 6, 14, 15, 18, 21, 22, 28, 44, 68, 71, 72, 75, 76, 80, 83, 92, 94, 96, 98, 100, 106, 108, 111, 112, 117, 142, 148, 152, 160, 163-166), from the Keuning-Tichelaar family (pages 4, 16, 19, 24, 38, 46, 49, 60, 62-64, 78, 168), from the Kaplanian family (pages 8, 10, 11, 172), by Avo Kaplanian (pages 90, 155, 157), from the MCC Archives (pages 116, 123, 126, 130, 135, 139, 146), supplied by Harriet Berg (page 138); all photos of quilts by Jonathan Charles.

"One refugee remembers" by Kate Good (page 124); "Centurion Martha Yoder still stitching for relief" by Harriet Berg (page 134); "About the Quilts" by Phyllis Pellman Good (page 180).

The quoted material on pages 23-25 and 42-43 is used by permission from *The Low Sky: Understanding the Dutch,* Schiedam Publishers. All rights reserved.
The quoted material on page 40 is used by permission from *Searching for Anne Frank; Letters from Amsterdam to Iowa,* Harry N. Abrams, Inc. All rights reserved.
The quoted material on page 41-42 is used by permission from *A Short History of Amsterdam*, Bekking & Blitz. All rights reserved.
The quoted material on page 133 is used by permission from *The Earth Is the Lord's: A Narrative History of the Lancaster Mennonite Conference*, Herald Press. All rights reserved.
The quoted material on page 137 is used by permission from *Up from the Rubble,* Herald Press. All rights reserved.
The photographs, other visual materials, reports, and letters from the Mennonite Central Committee (MCC) Library and Archives are used by permission of Mennonite Central Committee.

Design by Dawn J. Ranck

PASSING ON THE COMFORT

Copyright © 2005 by Good Books, Intercourse, PA 17534
International Standard Book Number: 1-56148-482-2
Library of Congress Catalog Card Number:: 2005001932

Library of Congress Cataloging-in-Publication Data
Keuning-Tichelaar, An, 1922-
    Passing on the comfort : the war, the quilts, and the women who made a difference / An Keuning-Tichelaar and Lynn Kaplanian-Buller.
       p. cm.
    ISBN 1-56148-482-2 (pbk.)
    1. World War, 1939-1945--Netherlands. 2. Netherlands--History--German occupation, 1945-1945. 3. World War, 1939-1945--Personal narratives, Dutch. 4. Quilting--United States--History--20th century. 5. World War, 1939-1945--War work--United States. 6. World War, 1939-1945--Women--United States. 7. World War, 1939-1945--Women--Netherlands. 8. Keuning-Tichelaar, An, 1922- 9. Kaplanian-Buller, Lynn. I. Kaplanian-Buller, Lynn. II. Title.
    D802.N4K46 2005
    940.53'492'092--dc22   2005001932

Table of Contents

From An—To my children

And thank you to Lynn for the initiative, to Inge for typing, to Phyllis and Merle Good for publishing, to Anke for completing the project, and, above all, to Herman for the time it cost him.

From Lynn—To An, and to my mother who loves stories

And a thank you for your help and inspiration to Sheila Gogol, Donna Halvorsen, Bernadine Yoder, Lil Bartel, Lisa Friedman, Dave Worth, Brenda Wagner, Carolyn Beyer, Franciska Rosenthal Lowe, Liesbeth Ernst, Chaya Beckerman, Pauline Burmeister, Piet Visser, Anne de Jong, Mark, Paul, and Rachel Buller, and Phyllis and Merle Good. Special thanks to An and all her family and helpers, without whom there would be no book.

Avo, you are my rock, my mirror, my sweetheart. Amir, you're a dog.

We are donating a portion of our royalties to help establish an International Menno Simons Center Netherlands, or related efforts. Giving to others on principal, as well as to compensate for our personal shortcomings, is a theme in both our lives. By passing on the royalties, we wish again to pass on the comfort which has been extended to each of us, and which we have given each other through these stories.

—An Keuning-Tichelaar and Lynn Kaplanian-Buller

Lynn and An

About our stories . . .

This is a story with many parts and pieces, quite scattered in the beginning. Amazingly, the many pieces have come together to form a design that none of us imagined at first.

First there is An in Holland in the early 1940s, fighting to keep the War from taking over her young, promising life. Met with unspeakable horrors, she takes risks that would confound the bravest of souls. At the same time, groups of women across North America meet in sewing circles, making quilts—and then bundling them up and sending them off to do their part to give comfort and courage and respite during the War.

I come 20-some years later, showing up in Amsterdam in the early 1970s, a little rebellious and tired of another war. I didn't know An, and quilts were not something I ever made. But my grandmother and aunts, and other older women in my childhood church, did. And I knew an immigrant's longing for the textures of home.

We have scattered images of 19 quilts, which eventually emerge near the heart of this story, throughout the book. These quilts drew An and me to each other.

We'll put this story together a little like a quilt top—here a patch, there a patch, until the design emerges, startlingly cohesive.

Terrible odds. Determined women. Quilts, well-worn from having been called into active duty.

Lynn Kaplanian-Buller
Amsterdam, 2005

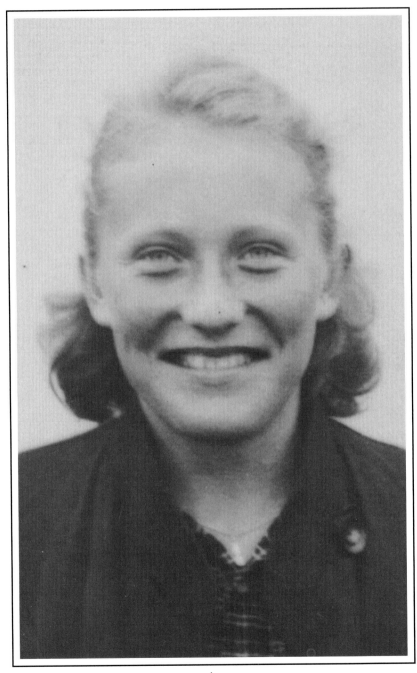

An

An—1944, Amsterdam
I begin my work with the Resistance

*O*n May 10, 1940, the German army invaded the Netherlands. They took over the country five days later, occupying Holland for five years. This tiny, densely populated country, with its tradition of independence, suffered hunger, unimagined hardships, and much death. Resistance groups began forming—at great risk for all who helped in the Underground.

The year was 1944. I was 23. I was beginning to do secret errands for the Resistance. This time I was asked to transport a Jewish baby from Amsterdam to Makkum, far in the north of Holland, in a big overnight bag. The baby had been given a shot to keep it quiet, but I am still nervous when I think about what could have happened. I took the boat across the Zuider Zee from Enkhuizen to Stavoren. I put the bag on the seat next to mine. No one sat down there. "I have such an unsafe feeling," I wrote in a letter to my good friend Herman. "It feels like something big is about to happen, but my package is very close by, so nothing can go wrong. Except . . ." And then a bomb dropped on the water. The boat suddenly started to tilt over and there were shots. Everyone scrambled to lie down in the aisle.

That is when I realized what had happened. The man sitting on the other side of me was slumping over in his seat, dead, and there was a hole in the scarf I was wearing! All I know is that I got the baby safely delivered to foster parents in my hometown of Makkum. But what would have happened if I had been hit? I took this as a sign that I was being asked to take on a larger task, and that I would be given the means to complete it.

Lynn

I wasn't sure why we had come. As we approached the idyllic country house over the only access, a bicycle path laid out of bricks, I wondered how the weekend would go, especially because we were bringing the only child. These gatherings of Palestinian students, all male, mostly Christian, usually centered on the menu. The guys had taught themselves to cook while studying and enjoyed (almost) nothing more than spending hours planning, shopping for, preparing home recipes, and telling jokes in Arabic together in a big kitchen, then eating it with their loved ones. Everything they did together—washing up and preparing coffee, too— was so in contrast to the usual image of Arab men that we women used to laugh.

If any authorities picked up these six guys for questioning, they wouldn't agree on anything politically, but they could recite—down to the spices—the complete menus of the previous week. Gentle, homey guys, they thrived on speaking their native language together, especially enjoying the intricate double entendres which Arabic provides.

The most far-flung of the group had been complaining to his fellow psychology students that he was missing his "brothers." One of their friends, after consulting with her parents, invited the student named Samir, to come to her parents' weekend house with all his Palestinian buddies and their families. So here we came.

Avo and I and our three-year-old daughter, Nadine, traveled up from Landsmeer, just above the Amsterdam harbor. The oldest of the student lot and the most settled, we both worked at demanding jobs and tried to bring Nadine up in the best of three cultures—Palestinian, American, and Dutch—mostly during evenings and weekends. We were tired constantly. Upon arriving, I was relieved to see that the farmhouse was large enough that I could peel off early to sleep next to Nadine if the guys started one of

Borg, where the group spent the weekend.

their all-night, low-stakes poker games. Nadine would wake early the next morning, of course, and it would be my turn to get up with her.

After seven years in the Netherlands, I still marveled at Europeans' ability to get together just to be together or to take a walk just for the pleasure of it. In Minnesota, we got together to Do Something Useful. Celebrations counted as a good reason, but there had to be a focus. And one went for a walk only to blow off steam, to cogitate heavily, or to get to some place specific. We would never just walk around together. Always eager to fulfill others' expectations, I often felt adrift in these gatherings of Palestinian men and European women, most of whom were still students. Added to this was my role as a working mother and I often felt somewhat confused about how I fit into these events. I learned to stop worrying about what others might be expecting of me and tried to do what made the most sense, while doing no intentional harm to others.

We walked into the farmhouse which had a huge open ceiling where the hayloft had been removed, and hanging on the wall was a quilt which

Log Cabin

looked very North American. The house was charming. Full of antique toys and built-in cupboards, it was warmed by a cast iron pot-bellied stove which threw off a cozy heat, necessary to counter the drafts which sneaked in around the poured-glaze windows. Some of the bedrooms, converted stalls, had very low ceilings. Others, up under the hayloft, were very high and long. As I walked through, my wonder increased. A handmade quilt covered every bed, and every closet held stacks of more folded quilts.

Who lived here? Where did these quilts come from? Who were these people? I asked Samir.

He thought the parents of his friend were a minister couple—Baptists, or something to do with Menno Simons. What? Menno Simons? That was a name I hadn't heard since my church instruction class in Mt. Lake, Minnesota. How could there be Mennonites way over here, and with such a long history? All I knew was that Mennonites had all been emigrants from colonies in the Ukraine, they all spoke a 16th-century Dutch/Germanic dialect, and they had come to North America to avoid being pressed into military service, based upon principals of non-violence set out by Menno Simons. Had they started a colony in the Netherlands, too?

A new chapter opened in my life. We had a lovely weekend. Nadine slept in the built-in bed closet, which was painted a lovely salmon-pink with turquoise trim. And when we arrived home, our son was conceived in the afterglow of a deeply pleasing day.

The quilts stayed in my mind. The week following, I tracked down the telephone number of the house's owners and asked Mrs. Keuning if it would be possible for me to purchase one of the quilts, explaining that they reminded me so much of home. Mrs. Keuning said that she couldn't sell me a quilt because they weren't her property, but that I could come choose one to have. I didn't understand her gesture—my knowledge of the Dutch language was not strong enough to pick up subtleties—nor did her offer fit into any imaginable context in my mind. I knew the price of quilts in quilt stores, and I certainly didn't consider just taking one from a stranger. Besides, if they weren't hers, how could she give one away?

Inside at Borg.

About 10 years later, I was busy thinking up ways to tell the story of Thanksgiving Day to the Dutch customers of our American bookstores in Amsterdam and The Hague. Quilting had become a very popular handcraft by then, and our store was an important source for Dutch women wanting to learn the patterns and history of North American quilts. Recalling the quilts in the farmhouse near Drachten, I called Mrs. Keuning again to ask if we could perhaps exhibit the quilts in the bookstore's art gallery. As I explained who I was, she interrupted: "Lynn! When are you coming to get your quilt?"

"I can't accept a quilt from you," I stammered.

"Well, why not?" she asked. "What have I done wrong now?"

"You haven't done anything wrong at all," I explained. "It's just much too large a gift to

Nadine in a bedstee, a bed "cupboard" built into the wall, at Borg.

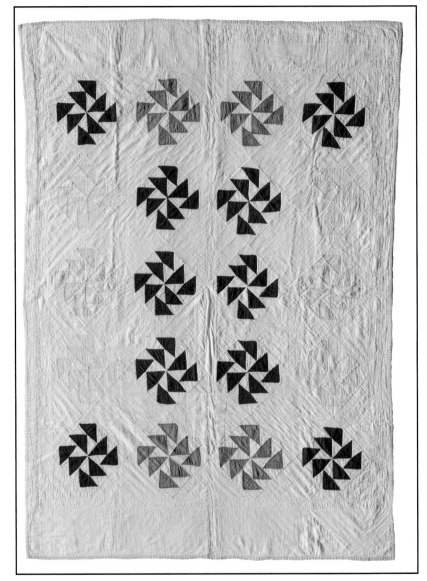

Dutchman's Puzzle

extend to a stranger, or to accept from a stranger. But would you consider showing the quilts at an exhibition? And coming for Thanksgiving dinner in the store? Perhaps we can get to know each other better."

An agreed.

A few months later, as she, her daughter, Anke, and I walked past the large store window hung with her quilts, she gasped. Later, she explained that the quilts had served as the sole keeper of her stories about all the struggles of the War years. When she saw the quilts exhibited in public, she felt freed to also tell her stories for the first time. Before she told others, she wanted to tell her daughter who, until then in 1989, had no idea of the part her parents had played in the Underground Resistance during World War II. Until that time, An had simply said that the quilts came to Friesland from North Americans as relief goods for the Europeans who had no blankets left after the war.

An and her husband Herman, their daughter Anke, and my family—Avo, Nadine, and Paul, now 10—ate Thanksgiving dinner together and learned to know each other a little bit. An and I felt a recognition and a friendship far older and deeper than was possible. It was a kind of comfort and a wordless understanding though we had just met, and she is 28 years older than I am.

I would not hear the stories, however, until much later.

An

An—April 1922-1937
A little background

*T*was born April 26, 1922 into a once quite wealthy family of ceramic-makers who owned a factory in Makkum, the Netherlands. In the late Middle Ages, Makkum was a harbor town where shipping and trade flourished and industry boomed. There were oil plants, sawmills, shipyards, lime kilns, and potteries. The residents were no longer primarily fishermen; many had become craftsmen. The owners of the mills and plants, artisans themselves, hired people to work for them and became respectable citizens and employers. Social relations changed. People became more articulate. They started to read the Bible themselves.

It was a time of criticism and unrest in the Roman Catholic Church. Radical believers were turning away and starting their own groups. They rejected the baptism of children and the practice of indulgences. The power of the Catholic Church's authority began to decline. In Witmarsum, near Makkum, Father Menno Simons (1496-1561) also left the church, joined the Anabaptists, and became one of their leaders.

Throughout Friesland in the north of Holland, congregations were formed that met in secret because of persecution. The groups were in contact with each other as sources of support and inspiration. Particularly in the countryside, there was a great deal of this kind of association. It is thought that while involved in these activities, Freerks Jansz, a farm boy from Jorwerd, met Jouwer Emes from Makkum, and that they later married. Freerks moved to Makkum, where there was already a sizeable ceramic industry in the 16th century. He

At the Makkum ceramics factory.

The Turfmarkt in Makkum.

set up shop as a pottery-maker and in the late 16th century became the founding father of the Tichelaar company. For centuries, the Tichelaars were staunch Mennonites and wealthy—until my grandfather invested the family fortune in Russian bonds in 1917 and lost it all.

Still a Mennonite but no longer wealthy, my father had to start over from scratch, but with the former economic and social standing still expected of our family. This was not just a case of family pride—in those days, before welfare benefits, people with money were expected to care for those without. If one of the town's regents dropped in standing, it meant a drop in security for the whole town.

I grew up in a sober household. We sensed that the outside world saw the name "Tichelaar" as a distinguished family who played a special role in Friesland. Because our family had provided town fathers for hundreds of years, my father, Jan Pieter Tichelaar, had much more influence in the village than an appointed mayor.

Our house was on the Turfmarkt. It was an old canal house with a corridor more than 20 yards long. I remember that this hallway was completely tiled, and in the wider part at the front there were tiles on both sides, composing biblical tableaux. On the one side was Moses and the Burning Bush and, across the hall, the Summoning of Abraham. (The funny thing is that even though I saw it every day, I always thought it was the Summoning of Mary. That story apparently appealed to me more.) With 39,000 individual tiles, this house is the most tiled house in the Netherlands and dates back to 1669. (Our forebears purchased it in 1696, and my brother, Pieter Jan, recently restored it to the way it appeared in earlier times—the front rooms to 1776; the garden room to 1731.)

On Sunday afternoons, when my father and mother listened to the concerts at the *Concertgebouw* on the radio, we played hide and seek through the house with our friends. The wrapping room was behind the kitchen. Huge bales of wool shavings were kept there to be used for packing the earthenware. The staircase went up from the wrapping room to the story where Grandma lived, my father's mother. She had lovely penmanship. Grandma wrote all the invoices with carbon paper, and they were copied by someone at the office into the big accounts receivable ledger. I loved Grandma a lot. She was a cheerful woman with a great sense of humor.

I don't know exactly how old I was when I woke up, and right in front of me I saw a big white ball of light in the sky. I was very scared and called my mother. When she turned the light on, everything was back to normal, but as soon as she left and turned the light off, I saw it again, even closer. I called my mother again. She closed the curtain. It was the moon. It was not until years later, when I was married, that I realized my dislike of the moon must have started then. Discovering this gave me some peace, but I am still a scaredy-cat, no matter how tough I might act in an effort to hide that and to try to belong.

In between two beautiful sisters, I was the ugly duckling, which was something older sister Betsy let me know in no uncertain terms for years on end. My mouth was too big, and I was cross-eyed and much too skinny. As an adolescent, I was really bothered about all of this. Fortunately I was somewhat distracted from these concerns when a baby joined our family in 1928. We all adored Pieter Jan, our bright and curious little brother.

School wasn't easy for me. After I was held back again in the third year of high school, I was given the choice of doing the year over again, switching to an easier school, or going to work for my father at the office.

I felt safe and relieved when I decided to go to work at the office. I spent three years there, from 1937-1940, and I learned a great deal. It seemed I hadn't failed at school because I was stupid. The reason was more that I was not functioning well physically. And I was always looking to see how Betsy was doing things. I wasn't mature enough; I didn't have self-confidence. It took me years to get over my sense of inferiority. I acted tough and told other people off—and I had a big mouth—so they wouldn't guess how inadequate I felt. I was always trying to prove myself, but deep down inside I knew it wasn't working. On the contrary.

While I worked in the office, I spent a lot of time with Grandma, who would prepare the invoices I brought upstairs as rough copies. I heard her talk about her life and her attitude toward society. I learned handicrafts from her—embroidering and crocheting. I still remember her telling me, "If you are alone later in life, you should still set the dinner table properly." That made an impression on me.

Tiled walls and fireplace in the Tichelaar family home in Makkum.

Left to right: An, her sister Betsy, her mother, Antje, and her sister Nel.

My faith was slowly starting to grow, side by side with all my doubts. I enjoyed my religious instruction class. I liked the stories in the Bible about special people. Florence Nightingale was also important to me. I idealized her. She was one of the reasons for my later career choice.

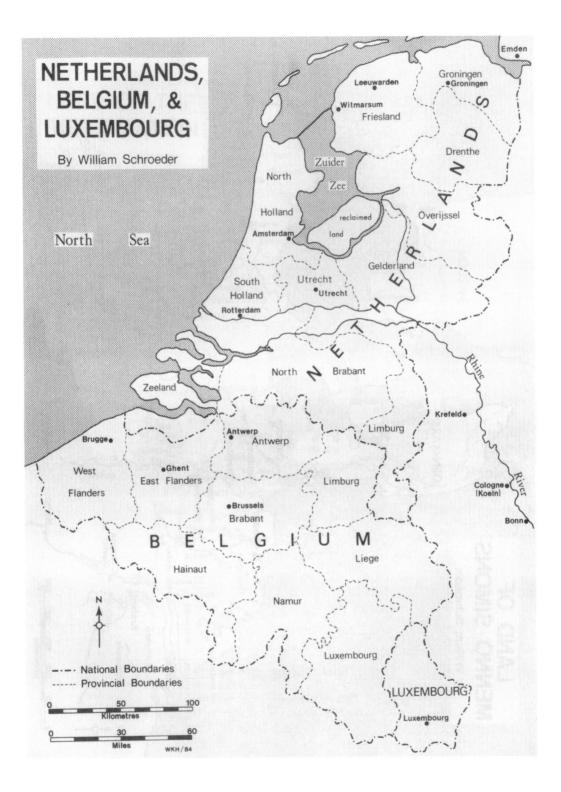

NETHERLANDS, BELGIUM, & LUXEMBOURG

By William Schroeder

Emden

Leeuwarden

Groningen
•Groningen

•Witmarsum
Friesland

Drenthe

Zuider
Zee

North

N E T H E R L A N D S

Holland

Overijssel

reclaimed
land

Amsterdam•

North Sea

Gelderland

South
Holland

Utrecht
•Utrecht

Rotterdam•

Rhine

North   Brabant

Krefeld•

Zeeland

Limburg

Brugge•

Antwerp•
Antwerp

West
Flanders

•Ghent
East Flanders

Limburg

Cologne•
(Koeln)

Flanders

•Brussels
Brabant

Bonn•

B E L G I U M

Liege

Hainaut

N

Namur

Luxembourg

−·−·− National Boundaries
------- Provincial Boundaries

LUXEMBOURG

•Luxembourg

| 0 | 50 | 100 |
Kilometres

| 0 | 30 | 60 |
Miles   WKH/84

An—April 1938-1940
The German Occupation begins

At our factory, like most everywhere else in the late 1930s in Holland, business was booming. Father was giving a lot of responsibility in the business to me. Despite the trouble I had at school learning my German vocabulary lists by heart, I had no trouble at all memorizing the more than 800 numbers of all our ceramic products.

Then came the year 1938. Hitler started making his influence felt abroad. Especially after the invasion into Czechoslovakia and the Crystal Night, I tried to imagine what could happen. I listened constantly to the news. This scary thing kept coming closer and closer.

Poland was invaded. But it was far away and in the other direction. I heard about Jewish refugees entering our country and about trains filled with children. Jewish parents were trying to get their children to safety. Who could imagine then what was going to happen later?

An

At the end of 1939, Holland began to mobilize. Our whole country turned to preparing for war. Old soldiers were called up and retrained, and industries adapted to manufacture wartime products. I was glad when an entire garrison of reserve troops were mobilized and were sent, along with Dutch officers, to Makkum to guard the huge dike and protect the old Zuider Zee area from flooding by the North Sea. If the Germans got control of the dike, they could hold our entire country hostage.

The officers were quartered in private houses. I was even happier when my mother told the officer assigned to our house that he could quarter his

The map is from William Schroeder, *Mennonite Historical Atlas* (Winnipeg, Manitoba: Springfield Publishers, 1990), 4.

PASSING
on the
COMFORT

An's brother, Pieter Tichelaar, outside the Tichelaar family home on the Turfmarkt.

family in our front room. Our family moved to the back of the house. The officer and his wife were young and had small children. I could go out with them and talk to people who were not just from rural Friesland in the north of Holland. It was a very special time for me. I was 17 and not accustomed to going out. Escorted by the young lieutenant's wife, I went to the Development and Relaxation evenings. I loved every minute I spent there. I learned about all kinds of things culturally and socially by going to lectures and plays and dance performances. It was wonderful, but in the back of my mind I was increasingly aware of what could happen and that we were living with more and more of a threat.

The war broke out on the nights of May 9 and 10, 1940. We heard airplanes, but otherwise, everything was quiet. Father knew that our whole village had to be evacuated to Workum or maybe even farther away. We heard he was not going to leave, and we wanted to stay, too. Father took his civic responsibility seriously and, besides, he had a factory to guard.

The town crier told everyone in the village to get out as quickly as possible. People were to put their names on their house keys and leave them on the porch of Turfmarkt 5, our house. I sat on the porch in the spring sunshine holding a big drawer. I was entertained by all the keys that had no labels on them. What would happen when their owners came home? The lieutenant's wife joined me on the porch, and we suddenly realized how quiet the town had become. We were filled with excitement—and uncertainty. She felt that especially because her husband had left in the middle of the night to man the fortress at Wons with his company. Nearby was the important Ijsselmeer Dike which our boys had promised never to give up.

Mobilization and Occupation —
What they meant

"On 10 May 1940, as part of the *Blitzkrieg* (Hitler's plan to take over all the countries surrounding Germany in one sudden campaign), motorized German troops invaded the Netherlands from the western front. Five days later, the Dutch armed forces capitulated. The Queen and the Cabinet had fled to London several days earlier, where they set up a government in exile. Hitler appointed the Austrian Nazi Arthur Seyss-Inquart as *Reichskommissar* in the Netherlands, to run the country now that the government had fled to England. His primary task was to reorganize the Dutch economy as far as possible to serve the war effort." *

Although there hadn't been much support for Nazism in the Netherlands before the Occupation, the Nazis did have four representatives in Parliament as members of the NSB, the National Socialist Movement. In addition, thousands of Dutch collaborators helped to secure and maintain the Nazi occupation of their country.

During the five-day siege in May, 1940, several thousand NSBers and Germans living in the Netherlands were arrested by the Dutch. Most of them were quickly released for lack of evidence. The Dutch panicked at the sudden invasion of German parachutists. Terror and uncertainty reigned. British citizens who had fled the Netherlands just in time, recounted, "On the first day of the invasion, parachutists dropped out of the sky like a vast flock of vultures. Most of them were disguised in Allied and Dutch uniforms; others came down in the uniforms of Dutch policemen and began to direct the population in the streets and mislead the army. One 'policeman' told a group of isolated Dutch troops that their friends were round the corner. When the soldiers turned the corner, German troops barricaded the road and slaughtered them. The 'policeman' was shot by troopers. But, most fantastic of all, the steward of the English ship said he and some of the crew had watched parachutists descend in women's clothes. They wore blouses and skirts and each carried a

* (See note on page 25.)

sub-machine gun. The steward could not tell if they were women or men disguised as women. Several eye-witnesses in the boat confirmed it and said others had come down disguised as priests, peasants and civilians" (*Daily Express,* London, May 13, 1940). Not knowing whom to trust set off havoc among the people.

"Hitler's national socialism was based on racism. The German people were superior to all the others. The Nazis, however, held the Dutch in high esteem. Seyss-Inquart found that the Netherlands was a very organized society. With the exception of the government, practically everyone had remained at their posts.

"There is almost complete agreement among historians today that most Dutch people adopted a kind of tactic of accommodation during the Occupation. They tried to continue their everyday lives as far as possible and adapted to the changing circumstances wherever possible. Only a minority chose either active resistance or full collaboration. The majority just let it happen.

An historical photo of Makkum

"With the government abroad, local Dutch officials introduced numerous new rules and regulations without any parliamentary procedure. Seyss-Inquart utilized this parliamentary vacuum to impose measures that allowed the Nazis to completely suck the economy of the country dry.

"Dutch workers were 'drafted' to labor camps in Germany to allow German men to be soldiers. The Dutch authorities generally cooperated in the selection of young men for forced labor in Germany. Eventually all Dutch men had to sign up. Having been self-governed for centuries, the Dutch had no distrust of the authorities. Used to decision-making by consensus after discussion, they were psychologically unprepared for a government whose dominance was all-powerful."*

* Hans van der Horst, The Low Sky: Understanding the Dutch (Schiedam, Netherlands: Scriptum Publishers, 2001), 156-164.

An—1940
The Occupation

The cellar in our house was converted into emergency lodgings for any number of people. The little windows looking out into the alley next to the house had iron bars on them. The bars had been removed from one of the windows so there was a way out if anyone needed it. I don't remember whether I also slept down there myself, but I do know lots of folks did, such as Rev. van Drooge and his wife and other notables who stayed in our village.

On Saturdays we had permission to go out to fetch bread and other food. The bread was on the shelves in the bakery. One Saturday a group of us came in through the back door. I was the last of the group, as usual. I suddenly saw an armed Dutch soldier running towards us. Then he jumped up on the stoop of the house on the corner and aimed his rifle. I saw an airplane behind the post office flying very low, I heard a shot, and the plane fell into the water. The soldier began cheering himself for his feat of bravery and for his very lucky shot to the propeller or fuel line. For a single moment I thought of the boys in the plane, but then I felt happy for the soldier who shot them down.

When I lay in bed that night, I was so confused. What was there to be happy about? I didn't know what to think. I couldn't fall asleep as I lay next to Tiny, the doctor's wife, that night. The doctor had been drafted and Tiny didn't feel safe in her big house in the middle of the village, so she had asked me to come sleep in her house.

The next night she woke me up in the middle of the night. We heard cars and music. And in the distance we could hear shooting from Kornwederzand in the direction of the Ijsselmeer Dike. It went on the rest of the night, and then all day with a certain regularity. That evening when the vehicles came into town, we saw that in fact, they were trucks. And in the clear moonlight we could see piles of bodies in all kinds of positions on top of each other, some of them shouting or moaning. In front of the trucks marched a soldier playing an accordion to drown out the terrible sounds. Aghast and appalled, we looked at each other and burst out in tears. We crawled into bed but we couldn't fall asleep. The same thing kept happening for several nights in a row. But after the war, we were told that only a couple of men had died.

Several years ago I spoke to the commander of a marine ship that had been in the vicinity. He confirmed what we had seen. Large groups of Germans rode horses onto the northern end of the dike in the direction of Kornwerderzand. As soon as these invaders were within shooting distance, the Dutch on board ship aimed careful shot and cleared the whole dike. All those who died there were young boys, driven to their death like cattle. Their bodies were removed at night; no one was supposed to know. At first, when this whole event was denied, I was very bothered about what I saw and knew. So I suppressed the memory as if it were just a dream. Nothing appears in the official reports about it. But finally this man confirmed what I saw—at least 500 young men were killed those nights.

There was a five-day war, capitulation, and then the German Occupation of the whole country including our village Makkum. Once Makkum was occupied, we had no more fighting there until near the end of the war. And, in spite of being occupied, the village, and our life there, returned nearly to normal. Our factory opened for business again. I worked at the office, just like before. Things changed very slowly. The German officers were interested in our factory. In fact, they wanted to buy it. We still had a lot of earthenware items in our second attic, mostly with imperfections. One day when my father wasn't home, I sold at least half of those items to the Germans. They had seen the perfect items in the factory, but they didn't see the difference in the things they bought. I was very proud of this transaction. My father was quite surprised, and he wasn't sure whether he should compliment me or not.

I wondered what our future was going to be like.

Lynn

Lynn—1949-1972
From Heron Lake to Amsterdam

I grew up in Minnesota in a small town on the wide prairie. The snow sometimes fell 12 inches deep overnight and the Alaskan wind blew straight down to our front door. We celebrated the first centennial of statehood in 1958, pioneer memories still alive within the small-town city halls and the old men who filled the benches in front of them daily.

Most of the families lived a mile apart on mile-square sections of land, at least a 15-minute walk to the neighbors in clear weather. Most everyone's time was spent at home on the farm. Television was meager and not everyone had one until the mid-60s, but most houses had a radio, as well as a piano or violin for homemade entertainment. People read eagerly. Philanthropist Andrew Carnegie had spread public libraries all over the small and bigger towns of America, which opened the world to the wide-open spaces.

The winters were long; the ground froze continually from November till mid-March, sometimes at 30 degrees below zero. People still worked outside and traveled, all wrapped up, in the cold to school, church, and stores. It was a hard life, where men and women worked as partners within well-defined roles to keep their families going, where neighbors and families helped each other and kept each other in line. These are my home folk.

My parents were teachers. My father ran the stringed instrument program from grades 4-12; my mother substituted as needed for English, history, or biology teachers out sick. We rented space for a huge garden from a farmer just down the road and grew all our own vegetables. We froze and canned them and ate from that garden all year long. My mother baked fresh rolls for Sunday breakfast and bread for the week every Saturday. A handyman or cleaning lady was never seen at our house—

Lynn, growing up in Minnesota.

not for want of one, but because everyone was expected to clean up their own mess, competent or not.

As the second son of a Mennonite couple from Mt. Lake, Minnesota, my father much preferred to play the fiddle than to help his father and older brother with carpentry or day labor. Visiting teachers from Bethel College in faraway Kansas heard him play the violin and plucked up my father to study music at the college. There he met my mother, a gifted local farm girl. She wrote poetry, studied journalism, and sang soprano well enough to want to be an opera singer. Instead, she took a position as a teacher in wild western Kansas, where her pupils ranged from six to 16 years of age, and she taught them all together in a one-room schoolhouse.

The United States entered World War II, and my father had to report for military duty. He registered as a conscientious objector based upon his religious belief and was assigned to alternative service in a psychiatric hospital in Ypsilanti, Michigan. My mother followed him and worked there, too. They married December 3, 1943 without the presence of her mother, who thought Victor Buller a coward for not going to war. Grandma ignored the marriage until my birth, but Grandpa came alone to the wedding by train. My father's parents came, too.

After serving in Michigan, my parents were posted to Puerto Rico where they did development work with Mennonite Central Committee (MCC, a North American relief organization), and to Mexico, where they helped set up a school in Chihuahua. Dad received a telegram in 1945 that his mother lay dying of a brain tumor, so they returned home by banana boat and train, arriving just in time. The War was just over, so they found teaching positions in a town nearby and settled into home life.

Four years passed before I came, the first redhead in either family. They were crazy about me from the start and moved from the upstairs apartment to a larger rented duplex. This house on Burlington Avenue in Worthington, Minnesota, had a deep garden full of peonies, jasmine, and mock orange bushes, as well as a sandbox in the back yard, protected by pungently sweet, blooming lilac bushes. The house had its own water well like most houses there, and the pump in the garden was a ready source of cold, clear water whenever anyone was thirsty. A tin cup hung on a string and everybody used it.

Dad taught me to play the violin as soon as I could hold the instrument. Mom read to me for a half hour every afternoon before our cozy nap. We went to the library together every week and always borrowed as many books as we were allowed. Mom read fast and hard, and so did I. We read so fast that we read each book three or four times before returning it. Mom's mother, finally accepting reality, sent me costume dolls from all over the world, as well as 78 rpm records full of classical music and folk stories.

Dad dreamed of starting a string orchestra and often invited musicians over to the house to play string quartets. I always went with my parents to the concert program they subscribed to. Every season brought professional music, dance, and theater programs to the prairies. From the time I was four years old I sat between them, Mom and I in matching black velvet and blue taffeta dresses, soaking it all in.

My brother Mark arrived when I was six, totally unnecessary in my view. Weren't the three of us a happy little family? I wasn't mean to him, but I did ignore him pretty much. When I heard he was coming, I imagined myself as a calm, nattily clothed and hatted big sister with a picture-perfect brother to complete my grown-up image. I would be a grand dame of a big sister, deigning to help him, but certainly in no need of anything he might have to offer. Sister Rachel arrived two years later, and brother Paul after another two years. By now I was totally outnumbered and did my best to share my parents' scarce attention by becoming The Big Helper. I also, it must be said, loved and really enjoyed The Kids.

Once in the winter, walking home across the snowy back field at suppertime, I caught my boot in a rabbit hole. Snow got inside and melted, then quickly refroze, enclosing my foot in ice. Unable to bend my ankle, I was stuck out there, the wind growing colder and stronger as the sun set huge over the white horizon. I yelled, but I was too far away for anyone to hear me. Finally, a mom who was cooking supper noticed that I hadn't moved for a very long time. She came out and rescued me and brought me home to my parents who hadn't yet missed me but laughed with joy to get me inside.

All of us kids helped at harvest-time. Farmers' wives with billowy bosoms wearing floral, belted dresses and ugly shoes were forever calling up to offer excessive apples, pears, plums, crabapples, rhubarb, red currants, black currants, raspberries, strawberries, tomatoes, and zucchinis to our largish family, if we'd only come and get them. Going to collect the produce was just the first step, followed by endless communal washing and paring, digging out the worms and the moldy parts, cooking the rest up for jam or preserves, or making a pie on the spot so that none of the fruit would go to waste.

We ground up green tomatoes after the first frost to make hamburger pickle relish. We scraped scalded corn off the cob into a huge mountain of milky kernels in the middle of the table. Mom scooped the kernels into plastic boxes and took them to the local locker plant where we rented freezer space. When you wanted your food, you had to go up on a high ladder with a basket on the front, use your own special key to open your locker door, then, wearing gloves, pick out the vegetables and meat parcels needed for the coming week.

We bought our beef by the half or quarter. It was delivered wrapped in white butcher paper parcels, the name of the cut scribbled with black wax crayon on each piece. Sometimes we knew those cows; generally we just knew the farmer who sold a few acquaintances a cut of beef.

Triangles and Hexagons

When fruits were in season from warmer climates, Mom always bought them by the caseload. Bushel baskets or flat trays filled with apples, peaches, apricots, plums, and cherries took turns sitting open in our cool basement. We were encouraged to eat as much as we liked as long as we washed it first. If any fruit was left by the time it got really ripe, we helped Mom can it for the winter so we could enjoy it months later.

My days were filled with school, music lessons, church, reading, helping Mom, and wondering aloud with Dad. I was growing up fast in lots of ways, had a strong, little body, and a fast, funny mouth. I had no fears. The world was safe, the future wide open "to the richest, most educated generation the world had ever known," as we were constantly being told by our teachers.

Then a neighbor man asked me to become his secret girlfriend. Although he didn't hurt me when I said, "No," I felt like a freak to have attracted him to me at age 10. I was indelibly marked by the experience. I came to believe that I was not like the rest of the kids, that I would never fit in. I would either have to pretend away the parts of me that were "Other," or leave. My childhood ended that day. The next day I began to get ready to survive a life outside the village, where my marking wouldn't show.

Dad's theological ties were to a Mennonite church in Mt. Lake, an hour's drive up the two-lane highway. Mt. Lake was a settlement where 19th- and 20th-century Mennonite immigrants had collected. I believe there were then seven different Mennonite churches in the village, population 2,000. Most of the village spoke 16th-century *Plautdietsch*, the language they had taken with them from the Netherlands when they emigrated to Poland in the 1500s and later to the Ukraine (called East Prussia). My dad and his siblings all spoke this language with each other, and it was the language used in church services while they were growing up.

We always went to Sunday school and church on Sunday mornings, either at the Methodist church at home in Worthington or, rarely, at Bethel Mennonite, an hour away in Mt. Lake. Mom never felt really comfortable among the women there, who also all spoke *Plautdietsch* and shared a friendly competition around household skills. They all sewed their family's clothes, baked bread, grew vegetables, cared for the sick, and were, in every aspect, good Christian women. And though our mother also did all those things very well, she never got into the competitive aspect of it. It had little value for her—she'd rather have been reading!

Dad felt his brothers and sisters never forgave him for choosing to do alternative service (because of his Christian pacifist beliefs) instead of military service during World War II, and it hurt him to his grave. They might never have understood him, but they did love him, that's for sure.

I studied hard, competed and participated in all kinds of musical activities (piano, organ, violin, and oboe), applied to go to Germany as an exchange student, went to theology camp, met lots of people from outside town. Chosen as a senior to tour Europe for six weeks with the School

Orchestra of America, I leveraged the selection into a better scholarship at Macalester College in St. Paul, said fond farewells to my high school friends in Worthington, and left, I thought, for the summer. It turned out to be for good.

While on tour in Europe, I received a letter in which my parents told me they had decided to move immediately to Duluth, way across the state, away from the prairie to a harbor city I'd visited once for a concert and had hated on sight for its grayness. When I got home I helped my family pack up everything I knew into a moving van. Then we filled the station wagon with cleaning materials and my belongings, and we family members piled in, driving off ahead of the truck. We dropped my things off at Macalester on the way up Highway 61 (made famous by Bob Dylan) to Duluth. I had a couple days before my orientation began to help my family get settled in. Then I went back down to the Twin Cities by bus and started college. I felt like I'd been wrenched right up and set back down on a hard flat space without roots.

I came home often at first on the weekends, but the whole family constellation had changed. When summer came, I moved out of the dorm into an apartment which seven of us girls shared, sleeping in the four beds in shifts, and got a job in the city. After the next school year, I took an apprenticeship job at Marshall Fields department store in Chicago and lived there alone for the summer. The following summer I stayed in St. Paul and worked at my best job ever—carrying mail.

After my third year at Macalester College, I quit. I was scared of what to do next and increasingly upset about what was being done in the name of nice American citizens to seemingly equally nice people in Vietnam. I became a community organizer with a peacemaking agenda, with sub interests in equal opportunities for women in the work force, in proxy fights, and in other uses of the economic system to help change public opinion. Our main actions were against a local producer of fragmentation bombs containing land mines designed to maim, not kill. (They're still being picked out of the rice fields of southeast Asia.) The organizing group where I worked thought up and executed public relations events to inform and persuade the public that their blind loyalty to government and corporations might need to be adjusted, that all was not as it seemed.

Lynn (right) at the table with her mother, Myrtle Buller, and with her sister, Rachel, in the lawn chair, at home in Minnesota.

The church had no place in my life except as a force for social change, although I'd been baptized in Dad's Mennonite church at age 15 after being chauffeured to weekly instruction classes in Mt. Lake by my dad. I agreed with the theology, had an emotionally moving baptism experience together with the rest of the 30 or so 15-year-olds in my instruction class, but didn't feel comfortable in the social life of the church.

Although we might have been theologically marginal Methodists and absentee Mennonites, we had lots of discussions about what Jesus might really have meant when he told parables and performed teaching miracles. My dad, who later found his other calling and became a Mennonite minister and church-planter at age 73, was an impassioned idealist and

Christ-follower. The man did not give up—not on God, not on human-kind, not on individual people. His standards were impossible to meet. For relief, he loved to tell jokes, play cribbage, or pick up the violin.

Curious, and tired of discussions which centered only around Jesus, I read and observed and got to know people of other faiths. I dedicated myself to social change. The people I worked with were wonderful and included an idealistic millionaire patron, a retired colonel, a radical environmentalist, two priests, a runaway rich girl, and a futurist who used to work with Buckminster Fuller.

Thousands of people were working together, creating new ways of community—cooperative grocery stores and people's health clinics were set up, we talked with the neighbors we previously ignored, and even organized street meetings which included the winos living across the street in the park. We challenged assumptions, learned to listen before labeling, and lived life intensely.

But at a certain point, I couldn't carry on anymore. I had a sense that I was telling an awful lot of adults what was right and what was wrong. At 21, I was a little short on life experience to be an expert. I, too, was not what I seemed. Some time out seemed to be in order, and my boyfriend Tim (son of the elderly radical environmentalist) had a plan. We would order a new Volkswagen van from the factory in Germany with money he had saved up, go get it, drive to India and back, then import the van as used and so avoid duties. It was all very legit and not unusual at the time.

I told my folks I'd be back in three months. My mother shook her head sadly and said, "You won't be." Mother was right.

We picked up the van in Germany and then drove west instead of east to see the tulips in Holland over Easter weekend. It was mid-March, 1972. I have never gotten to India. But I have spent most of my adult life in the Amsterdam area.

An

An—1940-1943
I go to the city

*I*n the fall of 1940 I went to Utrecht to study nursing. My sister, Betsy, was living there in the city in rented rooms. I lived in the hospital with the other student nurses, the youngest in a group of 12 girls. We all took part in a three-month orientation period.

The atmosphere at school was tough. The director was a difficult woman; she seemed jealous of the younger women and that made her cruel. My best friend, Mieke, and I didn't know how to cope with the director. We were having a hard time and we comforted each other.

After three months, we were allowed to go home. I said good-bye to Mieke. We were both looking forward to sharing a room when we returned to the hospital. But when I came back, Mieke wasn't there. I learned from the staff that she had committed suicide. I was shocked. She was my first real friend and now I was alone again.

That evening I watched out the window of the room I would have shared with Mieke. Slowly, I felt peace inside, and it was as if someone told me, "Yes, you can!" just like my mother had said to me several times before. I felt a hand on my shoulder encouraging me and making my self-confidence grow. From then on, I had a new view of my life.

As time went on, I found I wanted to talk with people who shared my beliefs. We didn't talk a lot about faith at home. I had been to instruction class and the Youth Circle, so the seeds were there, but they lay dormant in my field of indifference. Now I wanted to know more, to discover more. So I went both to Mass and to Dutch Reformed services. Mass seemed mystical and had a totally different framework than I had grown up with. I was fascinated by these churches, but after attending services at a number of them, I realized that if I were to belong anywhere, it would be with the Mennonites.

The only person I could talk to about this was Uncle Tonnie, my father's brother who was a Mennonite and a warm spiritual mentor. The

War, the persecution of the Jews, and everything that had to do with these terrors gave me serious doubts about faith. I no longer felt any certainty about my religious beliefs. At least I could discuss my thoughts openly with Uncle Tonnie.

Persecution of the Jews in Holland

As soon as the National Socialists took over the German government in 1933, they started to enforce policies meant to isolate and then exterminate Jews and other non-Aryans like gypsies, as well as "undesirables" like homosexuals and the mentally challenged. Sensing danger, many German Jews fled to England, Switzerland, the United States, and Holland. Anne Frank, whose diary illuminates her life in hiding in Amsterdam, was actually not Dutch. Born in Frankfurt, she and her family were German nationals until Hitler stripped all Jews of their citizenship. Anne and her family came to Amsterdam in 1933. After the Occupation began in 1940, German Jews in Holland had to register with the Office for Resident Foreigners. Bit by bit, the Jews were separated from the rest of the population.

"In November (1940), Jews [in Holland] were no longer allowed to work in government jobs or at universities. Books written by Jewish authors were banned and removed from schools and libraries. Jews were even afraid to keep these books at home in case the premises were searched by the police. In January, 1941, Jews were forbidden to go to the movies. Jewish musicians were not permitted to perform in orchestras subsidized by the government or to eat in restaurants. By May the Nazis forbade Jews to use public swimming pools or go to zoos or parks. After the 1941 summer vacation, Jewish children were no longer allowed to go to public school. They had to attend special Jewish schools. They couldn't visit Christians at home. By September, every Jew over the age of six had to carry an identity card displaying two photographs and stamped with a large black 'J.'"*

Rations in Holland

April 10, 1945

(Daily calories for a healthy adult are generally considered to be 2,500-3,000.)

October 1944	1,500 cal.
November 1944	950 cal.
December 1944	550 cal
January 1945	400 cal.
February 1945	320 cal.

. . . and today . . . reports that rations have again been halved!"

(MCC Archives)

"When war broke out, the Jewish community in the Netherlands comprised about 140,000 people. Most were descended from refugees who had fled to escape persecution in less tolerant countries. The Dutch Jews knew they belonged in the Netherlands . . . and never had any reason to distrust the Dutch government . . . not even when it issued the Aryan Declaration. Not when it fired all the Jewish civil servants—at first, on full salary. Nor when it dismissed all the Jewish teachers and gave them new jobs at special Jewish schools. The Germans devised a way of acquiring the Jews' property without too many problems by forcing them to transfer it to a special Jewish bank [which they controlled]. With the cooperation of local authorities throughout the country and under the supervision of the Dutch police, they concentrated the country's entire Jewish community in one area.

"The first round-ups of Jews took place on 22 February 1941 around Waterlooplein [in Amsterdam], the heart of the old Jewish quarter. The assault vans drove up, the Germans jumped out, grabbed the men, beat them up; it was as if they were hunting for

* Susan Goldman Rubin, *Searching for Anne Frank: Letters from Amsterdam to Iowa* (New York, New York: Harry N. Abrams, Inc., 2003), 32-37.

vermin. Four hundred Jewish men were arrested and deported to Mauthausen, where they were murdered. The response of the people of Amsterdam was the February Strike. For two days everyone refused to work or cooperate with authorities in any way. It was unique that the non-Jewish population should stand up for their Jewish fellow citizens. . . . Amsterdam was forced to pay a heavy fine. The Mayor and Aldermen were dismissed, the City Council disbanded. The will of Amsterdam to resist was broken and remained broken for a long time.

"The systematic deportation of the Jews began in July 1942. They were assembled at the Holland Theater building and were taken from there to Westerbork. From there, trains left every week for the concentration camps in Germany and Poland."*

"The pace of these measures was determined by how fast the death camps in Poland were able to 'process' those who were sent there. Of the 140,000 Dutch Jews—men, women and children—110,000 were murdered. This is 79%. In France and Belgium, both of which were occupied during the war, the percentages were 40 and 38 respectively. This is not because the Dutch were more anti-Semitic, it is just that in the other two countries, people were able to sabotage the Nazi extermination machine more quickly and effectively. There were protests against the persecution of the Jews in the Netherlands. The churches in particular responded very vociferously. But there was not enough practical, 'silent resistance.' When the Resistance Movement, inside and outside the Jewish community, began to set up escape networks, it was already too late.

"This does not detract from the heroic deeds of thousands of Dutch men and women who risked their lives or of the undaunted members of the Resistance who helped those pursued by the Nazis to escape or hide. Resistance groups specialized in finding suitable hiding places for Jewish children. Their parents gave them to strangers for safekeeping outside the cities until the end of the war.

* Dr. Richter Roegholt, *A Short History of Amsterdam* (Amersfoort, Netherlands: Bekking & Blitz, 2004), 116, 119-120.

"In one area, the Dutch Resistance was far better organized than comparable movements in other countries—the publication of illegal leaflets, pamphlets, books and even newspapers. Towards the end of the Occupation, the circulation of illegal papers reached about a million a day, all of which were written, printed and distributed in secret. The punishment for the possession of illegal publications was imprisonment and internment in a concentration camp; for writing, distribution and printing, it was death."*

* Hans van der Horst, *The Low Sky: Understanding the Dutch* (Schiedam, Netherlands: Scriptum Publishers, 2001), 163-164.

An

An—1943-April 1944
Discovering the Resistance in Amsterdam

*I*n my third year of nursing school in 1943, I transferred to the Binnengasthuis, a hospital in Amsterdam. At first I worked on the Children's Ward. I hated it there. The children were kept in playpens and separated by glass walls from each other. Each window facing the courtyard had a big black screen standing in front of it, which kept out all clear daylight. When I was given my work schedule and the specific hours I was going to work, I was very frustrated. On the early shift, I had to start by polishing the copper faucets, doorknobs, and nameplates on the doors. Then I had to make breakfast and, after breakfast, bathe the children and get them ready for the day. The children made a lot of noise and were naughty. The head of the ward, who was essentially a pretty nice older woman, would walk past all the playpens with a big bread knife in her hand and a scowl on her face to make an impression and to get the children to quiet down.

Unknown to me, the director of this Amsterdam hospital was a Dutch Nazi. The atmosphere was terrible, with a lot of German officers hanging around, expecting special treatment and favors from the Dutch nurses. After my first three-month trial period, I told the director I wanted to leave. He said I couldn't. I had to choose between staying at the hospital or being deported to the Eastern Front as a nurse for the Germans.

In those days, every nurse had a trunk where she kept all her belongings and equipment, all of which she paid for herself. I could not leave without it.

A hospital is a closed universe with all kinds of things going on, very little of which ever makes its way to the outside world and vice versa. When the director wouldn't allow me to leave, I consulted Nurse Thyssen, a Mennonite woman who had been working there for years and appeared to have relations with the Resistance. I asked her to help me get out of the hospital. I couldn't just take my suitcase and walk past the doorman out the gate, because I also wanted to take the trunk with all my belongings. Within a few weeks, she took me aside and told me that one of the patients who had recently been brought in with a wound had to be removed immediately before anyone recognized him. Would I help him escape? I said I would.

A porter managed to get my trunk out of the building while the wounded man and I tied bed sheets together and climbed across the shallow space below the eaves. With our legs clenched together, and with me using two arms and him only one, we slid six stories down the sheets to the ground. And I'm afraid of heights.

On the ground, three men took charge of the wounded man, who turned out to be an important man in the Resistance. I leisurely strolled over to the home of Jan and Hiltje, as if I had just gotten off the late shift. Hiltje was a girl from my village, living on Rapenburgerstraat in the Jewish district, who was married to Jan, a trumpet player she met during the mobilization. He was in the Resistance. I still remember how I crawled into bed with them and how warm it was there.

Jan picked up my trunk the next day. The day after that, I went back to Makkum to talk to my parents about what to do next. It turned out that Herman Keuning had already been talking to them.

Up north in Makkum, Rev. van Drooge and his family instigated a lot of social activities at the parish to bring some relief to the people who were in hiding. That is where I met Herman Keuning, a Mennonite graduate student who was hiding in the parish and helping out there. I liked him, but I didn't have any further interest in him in spite of the nice things various people said about him.

One time Herman came to Amsterdam with a special mission as an underground courier for Rev. van Drooge, and we arranged to meet at Formosa, a tea shop in Amsterdam. So it was in

Herman Keuning

this emotional atmosphere that we would meet and write to each other now and then. Herman and I continued conversing with each other through writing letters, but I was not in love. In fact, I was a bit uncomfortable, because he acted as if he was. We couldn't have any kind of relationship yet; I was not ready for that. I did mention to him that I wanted to leave the hospital permanently and do more work as a Resistance courier, but that I would need a place to stay. In his next letter, he suggested having a preacher take me into his home as a housekeeper so I could do Resistance work from there. I wasn't very enthusiastic about the idea of working at a parsonage, of all places!

With an address in Amsterdam, I could do Resistance work for the group operating out of Makkum. So I returned to the city—and I went to live in the home of a Mennonite minister in Vossiusstraat. I knew him from when he had served as the pastor in Makkum. As soon as I arrived at the parsonage in 1943, the family fired their servant. I was told that my job was to clean the whole house and cook for them. Every morning, the woman of the house came down the stairs with a book in her hand and asked, "You'll manage?" Then she took her leisurely leave. Once a week I scrubbed the outside staircase with its 24 steps. How I hated doing that!

Twenty-one years old, I was skin and bones. There was not much food for anyone, but even less for the new servant girl, fellow Mennonite, and a member of the upper class! By Christmas I had pneumonia and wanted to go home to my parents. There were several cans of Sanotogeen (an additive meant to strengthen the body) in the kitchen, so I borrowed one, knowing my mother would have some and that I could return a full can upon my return. Unfortunately, I did not mention this loan, and so, sick and starving, I was sent away for stealing food. And I wasn't given a ride from the south of Amsterdam to Central Station, either. It turns out that tasting the pudding while I prepared it, or eating an apple as a snack, was also considered theft.

My mother called my employers when I arrived home and told them my story. Although I didn't hear what she said, Mother returned to the living room with red spots all over her neck, and I knew she'd vented her anger at the woman of the house. Although Mother didn't want me to return, it was a point of honor with me as soon as I understood my employer's objections. So after Christmas I went back with a full can of Sanotogeen and remained there throughout the spring of 1944.

In Amsterdam, I had a food coupon route that took me to several addresses. From 1940 onwards, food and clothing, petrol, and all other necessities were not for sale on the open market but were rationed. One had to have ration coupons to buy any of these necessities. The Resistance used underground printing presses to make counterfeit ration cards, which they distributed to people in hiding so their caretakers could get them supplies. One Jewish woman lived way up in a tiny attic room on Ceintuurbaan in Amsterdam. She was a pitiful little old German-speaking lady whom I felt very sorry for. Whenever I brought her coupons, she tried to get me to stay with her as long as possible. I saw her loneliness and fear, which all the Jews were feeling, but I was helpless to find a solution. I understood that she had very little contact with the people who lived downstairs, who were being well paid for their "lodger." Sadly, her son couldn't come and visit her; he was hiding in Makkum. I used to stay and chat with her for a while because no one else seemed to be able to understand her.

Once when I came downstairs from my delivery, German soldiers were hanging around outside her door. A group of young Dutch girls walked by just then so I joined them, but the next week one of my other coupon addresses was raided. We were afraid someone had informed the Nazis about the addresses. Eventually the old lady was found and sent on the last train to Auschwitz. Of course she didn't survive; she was 94 years old. We were afraid she would betray the underground address of her son, who was holed up in the same place as Herman. Now and then she comes back to me in my dreams, and I see her standing in front of me, holding onto me and asking, "*Sie kommen zurück zu mir?*" (Will you come back to me?)

These were very anxious times. Lots of people were hiding out in Makkum: Jews, Resistance workers passing through, and men between the ages of 18 and 40, ducking forced labor in Germany. Many of those in hiding were students. Then something happened in Makkum that forced Herman and me to decide if we wanted a future together.

Jan Brouwer, a Jewish man who was hiding there, took Herman's bike without his permission and went to Bolsward. All the people who were hiding in Makkum could go out on the street there, but it was not safe to do that anywhere else. The police in Bolsward stopped Brouwer to check his ID papers, which he didn't have. So he gave them his home address and told them to call Rev. van Drooge. They did that, and Brouwer got very lucky.

Using Herman's papers, Rev. van Drooge was able to get Brouwer released as if he were Herman. The police accepted the story, but now Herman didn't have his ID papers anymore. That left only one possible option. Herman would start working for the church, file a report saying his papers were lost, and get new ones. As a preacher, he couldn't be sent to a work camp, and he wouldn't have too hard a time getting new ID papers. Identification papers were indispensable because without them you weren't eligible for food coupons. The police in Makkum knew him and knew about the papers he had "lost." They were very cooperative.

Herman had hoped that by helping Rev. van Drooge, he might get to do Resistance work. Herman also hoped to be able to finish his doctoral degree in theology. Many Mennonite pastors

Herman and An

worked in the Resistance. They sheltered members of the underground, organized and distributed messages and packages, spoke out in their sermons, thereby acting as examples for their listeners, and were an organizational home base for the Resistance.

So Herman started working formally for the church. But it was not easy for him to study because it was crowded and noisy at the van Drooge home, and the church was constantly calling him to help out or to replace someone. When working for the church turned out to be the only way to solve the problems caused by Jan, he temporarily had to give up the idea of getting his degree. Of course, he said he was willing to accept the consequences of a religious calling. Of course, he didn't realize at the time exactly what the consequences could be. It didn't sink in until the church started sending him to various parishes to preach, and people kept asking if he wasn't awfully lonely this way. Didn't he have a girlfriend? Was he planning to get married when he had a parish of his own? And a preacher all alone in a parsonage? That was *not done*.

Herman had another problem, and this one was his parents. They kept trying to convince him that I was not the right wife for him because I was not a scholar; I was not intellectual enough. But Herman was ready to get married—and doing so would both free him of his parents and save him from being alone in a parsonage. If he were married, he could be appointed as pastor in any of three communities.

Without telling me, Herman went to talk to my parents about his problems. They were both good listeners. Talking to them raised his self-esteem, it enhanced his sense of freedom, and it made him better able to make some real decisions. They advised him to first go and talk to me in Amsterdam.

We met again at Formosa Tearoom and this time sat there talking for a long time. I was overwhelmed. I did not feel ready to get married. I did not feel that practical reasons should be the *primary* reasons for getting married. We were being driven towards each other without being in love. Furthermore, we were too young to cope with a new marriage and the task of being a preacher and a preacher's wife. So what should I do? I empathized with him, but first I had to think about this whole situation. I had to think about whether I could deal with all this and whether it was what I really wanted. For a week, all these thoughts kept going around in my head. Then something happened that I felt showed me the way.

I was asked to carry the hidden baby from Amsterdam to Makkum—and the boat we were on was bombed and came under fire. When the man sitting next to me was shot dead and my own scarf took a bullet—but the baby never made a sound and we were both unhurt—I believed that I was being asked to take on a larger task and that I would be given the means to carry it out. Shortly afterward I was baptized and confirmed into the Mennonite church. And I agreed to marry Herman.

My conviction and sense of leading

One time, I biked home a different way than usual because I'd heard that the polder flowers on that route were so exceptional. On the way, I came upon a car parked in the middle of nowhere and a man who tried to wrest me off my bike. I resisted and got home safely, but I often had nightmares about the man following me and grabbing me by the shoulder. Much later, in 1979, I was able to ascertain that there were two hands on my shoulder, and that second hand has always been there to guide me as a positive force. This guide offered me assignments and the courage I needed to accept them.

My Resistance work developed naturally. My parents were active in the Resistance and supported my convictions, which were not motivated by politics as much as by humanitarian principles.

There is always a hand upon my shoulder. The surprises, the serendipitous experiences which happen in my life, are part of me. And they confirm my faith, even the negative surprises. I've always felt that my life had meaning, *must* have meaning.

My grandmother must have planted this idea in me but it became much stronger after my nursing-school friend took her own life. The evening before she did that was the first time I felt the hand on my shoulder. From that evening on, I felt that my life must count—perhaps even count double for my friend who hadn't been up to it. Her death gave me resolve to strengthen myself for the assignments I would face in life.

I had another scare on one of my excursions into Amsterdam when I had all kinds of things to drop off at different addresses. I had stopped at a house to give something to the people living there, and when I came out, there were two German soldiers on the stoop. I was scared, but I tried to hide it by cheerfully saying hello. (Resistance workers who were caught were summarily arrested and tortured before being executed.) I walked down the street, but when I got to the corner I noticed they were following me. I dashed into an alley and, from the corner I had backed into, I saw them walk by. I stood there for a long time before I worked up the courage to go back to my next address. Everything went okay after that. I didn't want to put my host family at risk, so I went to Rapenburgerstraat and spent the night there. When I went back to the parsonage the next day, my employers said they wanted me to go away for a couple of days. That was my chance to go home and talk to my parents.

I always thought it was very special and even a bit strange that my parents didn't object to my decision to marry Herman. After all, I had just turned 22. I asked my mother about it later. She told me they knew I would be able to cope.

I was scheduled to be baptized in March, 1944, but the service was postponed because my father, who was the chairman of the church council at the time, wasn't able to be there. Chief Dijkstra had arrested my father. His arrest was a big problem because our factory was full of fugitives. The three-story earthenware oven was not in use, but it sheltered a continual stream of people who all had to be moved elsewhere. Father was imprisoned at the Schotenshuis in Groningen for a couple of weeks. He didn't hear why he was arrested until after his release.

I was at home when it happened. I still see Scheepvaart, a *good* policeman, standing in the front hall to take him away. Father took everything out of his pockets and wallet; it was good he could do that. The chief didn't know he was active in a Resistance group. But Father was on pins and needles about what they did know. It turned out that the police chief had Father arrested for some minor offense, without telling us why or where, because he hated the aristocracy. In fact, the charge was illegal butchering! It could not have been any more absurd. Mother went to work with Rev. van Drooge, and they finally managed to find out where Father was. They got him released a couple of weeks later, using some smoked fish and earthenware as a bribe.

Once when I was looking for something in Father's desk after his arrest, I was surprised to see his Bible open at Psalm 27. That made a deep impression on me. We didn't speak much about religion at home, but it became clear to me then what an important part of his life it was.

After Father returned home, I was baptized on April 8, 1944, and he addressed me formally at the gathering that evening. I have forgotten almost everything he said, I was so emotional about the simple fact that he could be

SKETCH MAP
Location of
Mennonites in the
NETHERLANDS

...... International Boundary Lines
..—.. Province Boundary Lines

note – All places listed have Mennonite
congregations. Column line listing
for convenience only.

EXPLANATORY NOTE—The map of Holland printed here indicates the location of all but six of the Dutch Mennonite congregations, based on the "Doopsgezind Jaarboekje" for 1940, the official yearbook of the Dutch Mennonite churches. The map sketch was prepared by Henry Meyers, C.P.S. assignee, under the direction of the Relief Research Office at Akron, PA.

According to the 1940 "Jaarboekje" there are 134 organized Mennonite congregations in the Netherlands with 44,585 adult members. Most of these churches are urban and, very interestingly, vary in size almost in direct proportion to the population of the cities in which they are located. The largest congregation is at Amsterdam with a listed membership of 7,781. The membership of other leading congregations is as follows: Haarlem, 4,608; s' Gravenhage, 3,020; Rotterdam, 1,252; Leeuwarden, 1,250; Groningen, 1,142; Utrecht, 1,030; Arnhem, 912; Alkmaar, 912; Zaandam-West, 763; Aalsmeer, 721; Berg-Waal, 670.

A glance at the map will reveal that Mennonite congregations are concentrated in northern Holland, particularly in the provinces of Friesland and Noord Holland. These areas, although occupied, did not have to bear the brunt of military destruction as did the southern provinces. Mennonite church buildings and parsonages destroyed or severely damaged were all located in southern provinces of the Netherlands or on the estuary of the Rhine. Mennonite churches destroyed were at Rotterdam, Arnhem, Wageningen, Nijmegan, and at Vlissingen (Flushing); church buildings or parsonages were severely damaged at Aardenburg, Goes, and Heerlen.

there and do that. I was able to find a simple black baptism dress, and Grandma embroidered a lovely colorful blue decoration on it, so it was in the colors of the Mennonites. (Dutch Mennonite blue is a darkish, teal blue, symbolizing freedom of conviction.)

Avo and Lynn on their wedding day.

Lynn—1972-1974
Finding a home in Amsterdam

*E*ventually, it became clear that I needed a steady income; I thought that a job in a bookstore would be the thing. I could probably read for free, or at least cheaply. I started asking in every shop I passed. No luck. I spoke no Dutch and the shopkeepers all spoke English, so they didn't need me to talk with potential tourist trade. When my friend found a matchbook cover which read "American Discount Book Center," I got dressed and went looking for the place.

We found it on the Kalverstraat, Amsterdam's retail main street. I explained that I wanted to work in the bookstore, that I would work anytime and do anything, and that I had done some personnel administration and bookkeeping at my last job. After saying no three times, Mitch, a Charlie-Brown-like character wearing big brown glasses, finally paused after the bookkeeping information and, scratching his chin sideways, relented. "Okay," he said. "It would be useful to have someone to help guard the merchandise in the cellar shop on the weekends. Come in and work Friday, Saturday, and Sunday from 3-11 p.m."

"I'll be here," I smiled and thought, this is too good to last.

But it did last. . . . I'm there still.

One Sunday I came home after working the day shift to find the hall door of the dorm where I was living opened by a new person, a man with watchful dark brown eyes. Bald with a mustache and beard, he seemed ageless, with eyes full of hurt but a strong, young body. He didn't pay any attention to me, but I felt as if I already knew him. It took my breath away and I went to the kitchen to sit down. Avo was smart and funny and different, an orphan who was born in the Armenian quarter of old Jerusalem. He grew up in Amman, Jordan, and was taken in, along with his little brother, by family in Ramallah in the occupied West Bank of Jordan when their parents were both killed in a car crash. He'd come to Holland on a scholarship to study archeology,

Avo (right) and his brother, Mike

switched to cultural anthropology, and had done his master's research among Syrian nomads the summer before. Although our backgrounds were so extremely different, I felt safe with him, in the company of his sorrow. I could relax. He had mastered being marginal. A survivor who thought for himself, he wrote letters, lots of letters, to people he knew all over the world, including distant relatives in the Armenian and Palestinian diaspora. He kept the network alive for his brother and departed parents. Here was a man who loved to live—abundant with friends, respected at the university, his room was often full of people who needed to talk. But studying came first, and when he studied, the door was half shut.

Around us, people were getting divorced, not married. Masses of young people chose to live together rather than marry. But coming out of previous relationships, we both knew it would take all the means we could muster, as well as all the counsel of our friends and family, to help us to stay together in times of trouble. By marrying, we could formally ask them all to stand by us. We were wildly in love with each other, and we wanted to be together for a long time.

How long is long, and where would we live? Moderate Palestinians were suspect throughout Europe in those times and were being killed. We didn't want to settle in the Middle East. On my side, the war in Southeast Asia was still going on, and we didn't feel comfortable going to the States to live. Times were uncertain. Nonetheless, we decided to join hands and jump together into the future.

Upon graduating, Avo would have to leave the student house, but there wasn't room for both of us to live in the flat I shared. Unregistered for rental housing, we went looking for a flat. We found one to buy for such a low sum of money that we didn't even go look at it at first. When we finally did, we knew it was our place. But the bank wouldn't give us a mortgage because we were foreigners and likely to leave. A friend had offered to lend us money if we ever needed it, so I called him and asked to borrow $6,000. He said, "Sure," and with that in hand we persuaded the bank to give us a mortgage for $4,000.

Our wedding took place at Christmas-time so that my family could come during school vacations. They cashed in a savings bond and arrived on Christmas Eve, sleeping on the couches in our new living room. Dad and I went to the flower market and bought my bouquet. We went to City Hall by tram and Volkswagen Bug for the ceremony. We exchanged our vows and read to each other from Khalil Gibran's *The Prophet* in Dutch, Arabic, and English. My boss, Mitch, helped to sponsor the food and reception for about 60 people who came to our little apartment after that to eat and dance and make music. Avo and I and my family had cooked our wedding meal together

On the wedding day (left to right): Lynn's mother, Myrtle Buller; Avo's brother, Mike; Avo; Lynn; Lynn's witness, Anthony Cowl; Lynn's father, Victor Buller.

days ahead of time, preparing a buffet of pineapple-glazed ham, lambs' brains, lentil soup, potato salad, grape leaves, and carrot sticks. Our Persian friend sang a love song, drumming on an inlaid backgammon set. My sister, my dad, his German penpal, and I played string quartets. Dad and Horst had been corresponding since 1938 but never met each other until our wedding on January 2, 1974. Dad taught the whole crowd to sing "Chattanooga Choo-Choo," complete with hand motions. It was the perfect party.

Avo's cousins emerged from all over the world and came to Amsterdam in the months that followed. My Minnesota friends stopped by, my sister came over the summer after graduating from high school, my father wrote me a letter every week, and Mom penned a note on the bottom. Avo's new work included visiting all the Arabic-speaking social clubs in his function as director of the Foundation for the Well-Being of Foreign Workers. In typical Middle-Eastern style, members would show up unexpectedly at our door with gifts, to show respect by a visit or to consult him on some matter too personal to be discussed at the office.

Not nearly as sociable by nature as my husband (like my mother, I'd often rather be reading!), I worked out a way with Avo for me to remove myself honorably to another room after offering something to drink to our guests, and agreed ahead of time when to re-enter and claim him back when it was time for the guests to go home. We wouldn't have gotten any sleep otherwise.

Bookstore partner Mitch had been given an offer to swap bookstores while home in the States on a buying trip. I got a phone call from co-owner Sam saying Mitch wouldn't be coming back, but that he'd be sending someone else over soon and, in the meantime, just keep taking the money to the bank. A very successful businessman, Sam enjoyed building up his hobby store in Amsterdam. Hobby store or not, we were expected to make money every month and to put it in the bank. That became a habit which made it conceivable for us to take over the bookstores from him in 1983.

And so the years passed. Avo and I adjusted to life together in a third country, rich with friends and colleagues of all sorts. The guests at our table were always a rich variety. After the birth of our daughter, Nadine, we moved to a townhouse in an old village just outside Amsterdam.

Herman and An on their wedding day.

An—Spring-Summer 1944
Marriage in Makkum

There were three good reasons for me to get married. First, I would have a different name and would feel safer, because I had already been told that the police knew my name in Amsterdam. Second, we would live in a big house where a lot of people could hide. Third, I would be able to go on with my Resistance work.

When I was home at the end of 1943 and felt the wordless warmth of shared experience, I knew I wanted to have my life make a contribution and I wanted to act on the basis of my Mennonite background. I didn't feel like I was in love, but I sensed my feelings steering me in a certain direction that I never dreamed of. I was going to take a path with Herman. We didn't know what we were going to be confronted with along the way. But I agreed to marry him. We didn't expect much opportunity to get to know each other better while the War was on. Naive and idealistic, 25 and 22 years old, we decided to get married, taking a flying leap into the unknown.

We spent three weekends together before our wedding on July 27, 1944. On one of those weekends I was introduced to Herman's family. They invited us for dinner. We arrived just as the sun was setting. The food smelled delicious. He had told me his mother was a great cook, but when we sat down at the table after a very cool reception, Herman was given a hot meal and I was brought just two slices of bread. I was discovering right away what relations were like in this family. Herman didn't dare say a word; he just sat there nervously fidgeting with his dish and bashfully sneaking a look at me now and them. I felt sorry for him and began to understand a lot of his reactions, which I had been struck by, even in the short time I knew him. He was still a meek little boy who had to meet his parents' wishes, commands, and expectations. I couldn't be mad at him, but I was disappointed.

Herman's father worked for Shell Oil as a regional manager. His grandfather had been a large feed-grain producer and supplier. His mother ignored me. Apparently I was not her idea of a suitable wife for her studious son. My father and mother were both active in the Resistance so the two of them understood better what we were committed to.

Herman's parents tried very hard to prohibit our marriage because I hadn't studied enough, wasn't pretty enough, and probably also because his mother didn't want to let him go. They drew up a list of 10 points by which I fell short as a suitable spouse for Herman, and then sent the list to my parents. The bad relationship never changed.

Our wedding day began with rain, pouring on the roof of the verandah. Fortunately, the skies cleared and the mayor, a member of the National Socialist Movement, married us in the required civil ceremony at the Witmarsum City Hall. I don't remember what he said. We all went to City Hall in a bus running on wood gas. A little bit of gas had been especially saved up for our wedding car.

When we came back to Makkum, for the religious ceremony, a lot of people were already at the church. A public wedding was a rare occurrence at the time; a lot of people just got married very quietly without any fuss. But the church was packed. Two horse-drawn covered wagons had even come from Harlingen, where Herman had been active doing youth work. They were filled with conscription-age youngsters. Fortunately, none of them were picked up.

Herman and An

Herman's mother (second from left) and father (third from left)

The only place they could sit in the church was on the rafters or on the little balconies. I found it all very overwhelming and unreal.

After the service, we walked home. By now it had turned into a beautiful sunny day. One of the people in hiding took some photos that give a very clear picture of the emotions we were all feeling that day.

That evening we dined at The Prince. Our friends and families had collected coupons from everywhere so we could have a good meal. Fried and stewed eel—a big treat for everyone—were on the menu. Bouma, the innkeeper and cook, made a grand feast of it. Since orders were suddenly issued that day that everyone had to be inside by eight in the evening, Herman and I couldn't stay until the end of our reception because we would be driving some distance. Both of our fathers made speeches to us. Then we had to leave. I still remember how I felt. I couldn't say a word, but I knew this was a kind of farewell from my parents' home where I had felt so good and so safe. I still get that same feeling when I visit my childhood home where my brother, Pieter, and his wife, Joyce, live today.

The bridal party

Herman and I took a taxi to Irnsum where we would live. We were going to take along a radio, which we actually should have turned in, and our suitcases with our remaining clothes. Our pages, Pieter and Rob, were supposed to see to everything. But when we arrived in Irnsum, none of our baggage was there. We didn't have a telephone yet, so we used the neighbors' phone. I told my father that Herman didn't have any of his clothes and, as if it was the most normal thing in the world, that we didn't have the radio either. That definitely was not something you were supposed to talk about over the phone. I was clearly confused and forgot I was putting my family and our new neighbors at risk. Lots of people were picked up for less than possessing an illegal radio and jailed or sent to work on the East Front or worse.

We hadn't gone into our house yet. We were so nervous, but we finally did go inside, only to get the shock of our lives. My sister, Nellie, had helped us fix up the whole house according to our own tastes, but Herman's parents had come in the meantime and changed everything. I knew immediately that they had done it because of the doilies on the armchairs and side tables and other details like that. The whole atmosphere was different. Distraught, we looked at each other. They meant well, but what they did had the opposite effect. I felt so wronged and offended. Herman was confronted with "them against me" again. That was all he could say.

Hand in hand, we walked out of the house into the beautiful evening. We tried to cope with our disappointment and rage. We felt powerless; it seemed we had to accept a pattern we could not change. We slowly calmed down. I was able to listen to the silence again. The cooing of a pigeon in the apple tree was the only thing we could hear. The street was totally silent because of the curfew. Night fell and the mosquitoes started biting, but we weren't ready to turn in yet. We had not found what we expected in our house, and maybe we were afraid to spend our first night there! We still felt the tension that had built up over the past few days.

Bashfully, we climbed into bed. It was not until Herman touched me that everything I was holding in suddenly came out in a burst of tears, and Herman did not know how to deal with that. Inconsolable, I fell asleep—until a big bang suddenly woke me up. The bed had collapsed! It was a little joke on the part of the carpenter, who purposely had improperly fastened the supports holding up the spring mattress. A fun way to celebrate our wedding night! After I caught my breath, I was able to laugh about it. I could imagine Herman going the next day to the carpenter, who was also a member of the Church Council, and asking him for some nails. What a laugh he and his friends would have on us. We had met their expectations perfectly. Lying on the floor, we went back to sleep, totally relaxed now, cuddling up to each other. When I got awake, I saw Herman get up—wearing my flowered pajamas because he didn't have any clothes of his own there! A ridiculous sight but an entertaining way to begin the day.

For our honeymoon, we were going to row to the beautiful farm on the Wijde Ee where Herman had been a camp counselor. I found it hard to put the oars in the water at just the right angle and then to start rowing. I discovered Herman was a completely different person in the water—very direct and confident in a way I had never seen before. Not that I wasn't happy with this side of him, but it was so completely new that I was a bit shocked. It took me some time to get used to his quick commands and instructions. I still had not quite recovered from everything we had been through, and every so often I found myself on the verge of tears.

When we landed on the island, a group of kids were doing gymnastics in the barn. They challenged me to match their tricks, which I happily did, when suddenly the ring at the top of the rope came loose. I know I landed on the dirt floor with a bang, but I do not remember how I was moved outside and came to be lying on the grass. I lay there for four hours, unconscious. By the time the family doctor came from Grouw in another rowboat, I was just recovering consciousness.

Because of that delay, we arrived much later at the farmhouse than we had planned. The farmer's wife had left some food for us. We were tired and wanted to go to bed early. Filled with eager anticipation, I climbed into the bedstead first, but I didn't even notice when Herman climbed in beside me. Suddenly it was the next morning and we had allowed another opportunity to make love go by. I was so absolutely exhausted that I did not even realize what had happened.

The next day, we went rowing again, and finally, in a haystack, we made love as carefully as possible. I was very hesitant, but I didn't want to disappoint Herman. It was an odd beginning. We enjoyed the rowing and the freedom and the space all around us. Now and then we heard English fighter planes high above us. Fortunately we were hidden because they shot at everything they could see.

It was to be years before An knew that her fall in the barn had cracked two vertebrae. No one believed she had really been hurt, and so she walked around with the injury, increasing the pain and damage. She spent a total of three and a half years on her back over a period of 14 years, had four operations, and was reduced in height by three inches. None of the operations were paid for by her insurance or the Mennonite pastors' support fund because the accident had happened during the first two-week waiting period as part of her insurance coverage through Herman's policy. Everyone assumed that since she was a Tichelaar, her family would help them pay the expenses. In fact, it took 30 years for them to repay the loan for the hospital bills.

An

An—Summer-Winter 1944
Daily life in Irnsum

erman and I settled into the parsonage in Irnsum. During our first few weeks, there was a death in the congregation. Herman had to do the funeral, and I went with him to the family's home to pay our respects. They lived in a tiny house on the outskirts of the village. We would visit with the family in the front room, but first we had to go to the room in the rear where the body lay. The hot summer sun was beating down on the windows right next to the open casket. Everyone clearly expected us to look into the casket. We stood at opposite sides to view the deceased. All I saw was a swarm of flies.

I was so taken aback that I fainted and fell over the corpse. It was not until 14 years later that I found out why. It had to do with the tumble I took back in that barn! Fortunately, I regained consciousness almost immediately. (The family assumed I was pregnant, but that didn't happen until nine years later.) Despite my pain, I had to walk in the procession to the churchyard a few days later. Herman walked up ahead, just behind the coffin with the men following, two by two. The women walked behind them. Everyone was dressed in black. Herman wore a black suit and a high top hat and I wore a black veil. The old customs slowly disappeared after the War and it was no longer necessary to wear black, though I still do, even today.

As the pastor's wife, I had to chair the Sisters Circle, a group of women all much older than I was. It was my job to begin with a meditation on a passage in the Bible and then lead the hymns and prayers. I had never done anything like that before so I consulted my mother, who had the same responsibility in Makkum. Herman wanted me to do it for the first time in September. I dreaded the occasion, and as I was walking up the stairs in the church, I heard one of the women say in a loud voice, "What could a child like that have to tell us?" I dashed back home, but

* Because no
goods could be
imported
during the
War years,
the major
coffee and tea
packager
made pellets
from the dust
left from
the tea
which had
been stored
in their
warehouse.
This gave
hot water
a little color
and a
little flavor.

Herman was expecting something like this and he had locked the door. So I had no choice but to go back. It was something I couldn't get away from.

The women were sitting around a large table. I shook hands with each of them and sat down at the table. They were looking at me expectantly, and I told them what I had overheard on the stairs. "I don't have anything to tell you," I said. "I'm not trained in this. But I would like to hear from you what you expect of me." You could hear a pin drop, and then I said, "If you don't know what to say either, let's pray together and ask God for inspiration." They all looked relieved and put down their knitting and bowed their heads. I closed the meeting with the hymn, "Guide Me on Your Road," the only one I could think of. We each had a cup of surrogate tea,* and I asked them to go around the circle and tell me about themselves. When I was outside, I heard one of them say, "You never know, she might do." It is so typically Frisian to understate one's thoughts in that way. I was feeling better when I got home. With only a few breaks, I led the Sisters Circle at almost all the congregations we served until the year 2003.

When Herman and I were first alone together, we lived upstairs in a bedroom. We lit a stove to keep warm up there. Piet and Wim Meinsma lived across from us, above the De Zee family store. When we moved in, we visited them to thank them for making us feel so welcome. They proudly introduced us to their foster daughter, a darling Jewish girl named Eva ("Marijke" became her "Dutch" name) who had been hiding in one of their upstairs rooms for more than a year. She always had to be very quiet.

Piet and Wim did not have children of their own. With the store downstairs, they had to be very careful that no one could hear any noise from Eva. The little girl needed a bit of distraction now and then. She could look out the window and see a big farmhouse, and it was so far away there was no chance of anyone seeing her from there. Her main pastime was watching the patrol boat that sailed back and forth twice a day supervising activities on the Boorn River. She had made a special contact with the boatman. Uncle Fritz, a man in his sixties, waved to her whenever he passed by.

Piet and Wim became good friends of ours. Now and then Piet would get a special delicacy from one of the farmers and he always shared it with us. He called on January 6, 1945 to say they were having some problems, so we went straight over to their house. The sun was already set-

The neighbors' homes across the street from the parsonage in Makkum.

ting. We walked up the stairs, and when we got to the living room we saw two distraught women sitting next to each other with a child between them. I took one look and realized before anyone said a word that the one I didn't know was Clara, Marijke's biological mother. When Marijke was brought to the Meinsmas, they were told that her mother had almost certainly been deported, although no one was completely sure.

This was a big problem. Clara couldn't stay with the Meinsmas. Another address had to be found for her. I didn't hesitate. In a purely practical sense, it was the simplest solution. She would stay at our house and say she was Herman's aunt from Arnhem, because we didn't want her to always have to hide. She could walk in and out of the house, and as Herman's aunt no one would think anything of it. Besides, Herman had dark curly hair so it wouldn't be hard to believe.

It was hard for Clara Cohen to adjust suddenly to being able to walk around like a free person, but she got used to it. She would go shopping in the stores and regularly drop in at the house across the street. The

Meinsmas and we demonstratively read the same newspaper that Clara would go and get for us. No one had any idea who she really was.

In no time, our house was full of people in hiding, including children from the famine convoy, refugees, and evacuees from the western part of the country where food was scarce and living conditions were untenable for the infirm. Irnsum became an overnight stop for the organized transport of evacuees. Our living room served as a makeshift hospital, housing up to 20 sick, pregnant, or aged people. Most of them stayed one night before rejoining their groups to travel on by horse and wagon. But some were unable to go on right away and stayed longer until they recovered. One old woman died at our home.

Martien Postema was the first fugitive, in September, 1944, followed quickly by others. Martien and five of his buddies wired a canoe with a radio transmitter, and they would take it as far out into the Waddenzee as they could safely go, and send and receive messages from England. They were betrayed, so Martien hid out with us. About 16 years old, he shaved his legs and wore short pants to look younger, but as soon as he spoke it was clear he had a man's low voice. He was a danger to all of us as soon as he opened his mouth and so absentminded that he needed constant watching, no matter how old he was. (While with us, he devel-

The parsonage (far left) and the Mennonite church (far right) in Irnsum.

oped a plan to become a Mennonite pastor, which he later carried out.) Later, the son of the oldest Jewish woman to be transported to the death camps also hid at our home. I had delivered food coupons to her in Amsterdam.

Groups arrived in Irnsum every other day. I couldn't manage it all on my own, so I scheduled six teams of two girls each who rotated daily, to keep watch and help with the wake-up and departure of the fugitives.

These village girls sometimes took the opportunity, while being away from home for a night, to entertain their boyfriends briefly at the parsonage while their teammates covered for them. A local constable showed up sheep-faced to announce that he and one of the girls needed to get married fast. Since it had all happened right there in our kitchen, they thought it only right to ask Herman to perform the wedding, even though they were not Mennonites! I told them, "Go get married in your own church, be happy, and don't worry about etiquette."

We gave the travelers sandwiches for their journey. And we were given food coupons for the patients in our makeshift infirmary. Clara, our Jewish refugee, used every chance to make enough food to feed the starving folks who arrived when we weren't expecting any visitors. In addition, we had mysterious guests who got as little attention as possible. Usually they came in the middle of the night and left soon again, silent and nameless.

Because there was so little food left in the cities, a network of foster families in the countryside was organized, mostly by churches, so that at least the children would have food to eat. Most of the children's convoys arrived at night because of shelling by the English during daylight. The floors of both our attics were covered with thick layers of hay provided by the evacuation committee. The hay needed to be regularly replaced because of vermin left behind by the sleepers. The committee got the hay from the neighbors and brought it to the parsonage. One attic was for the children, who usually stayed for a night, and the other was for the irregular visitors, refugees, or other travelers, who stayed one or two nights.

Every children's convoy meant a lot of work. Before the kids went to their guest families, they had to be washed, checked for vermin, and sometimes treated with pesticide. There were also the bed-wetters, who were sometimes returned to us by their foster hideout families like rejected samples. When that happened I tried to exchange one of our fugitive kids for a bed-wetter, if the children agreed.

Sometimes far too many children were left with us, but when we saw them blossom, the number was unimportant. I needed to get horse fat from the slaughterhouse in Sneek to make scurvy salve. I still remember the hospitality and warmth I got from the Mesdag family there. They listened and let me vent my feelings, which helped me gather new courage.

Fortunately, I could organize well, and Clara Cohen, our Jewish refugee in hiding, was a big help. She did whatever cooking needed to be done. And people took turns going with Herman to Grouw to have a washtub filled with mashed potatoes and cabbage. If any of it was ever left over, Clara always knew how to make something edible for the late arrivals. Every morning we put a big iron pan on the stove filled with watery milk and milled wheat. It needed to be stirred constantly while it boiled. Except for the smallest children, everyone was instructed to take turns stirring the porridge, including Martien, who of course, had to be continually reminded. He was so utterly absentminded. One morning I heard a rough shout in the living room. The pan with boiling hot porridge had tipped over, and Martien got a good bit of it all over his leg. I could barely cut off his knee sock. Huge burn wounds kept him in his chair for weeks.

When the household grew, we had to divide the tasks and make a duty roster listing everyone's jobs for every day of the week. After a slightly problematic period, the system worked fine. Sometimes there was a bit of complaining about guests who weren't on the list because they were just passing through. We jointly decided on the tasks for everyone, from the youngest children to the old folks. You could exchange with someone if you wanted, which led to ample discussions and bargaining. To keep the atmosphere positive, I learned it was important to keep everyone busy.

There was one job no one was interested in volunteering for: cleaning the outhouse. Instead of a toilet that flushed, we had only a barrel that had to be emptied regularly. The tiny outhouse was built against the rear outside wall of the house, and it had a low door through which the barrel

The parsonage in Irnsum.

could easily be removed. Once a week, the barrel was picked up and emptied by men who came by with a big wagon, since officially it was only Herman and me living at the house. But since the house was usually full of guests, the barrel had to be emptied twice a week, and sometimes an extra third time. We didn't dare make the men with the official wagon suspicious. So emptying the barrel was an important job for the four oldest boys, and it had to be done right. The boys would take the barrel out to the Boorn River behind the houses across the street.

None of its contents dared spill. The barrel was heavy and hard to carry, yet it had to be carried across the street without anyone seeing, especially since the people who might catch a glimpse of it could be our enemies.

There was a curfew from eight in the evening until six in the morning. While the barrel was being emptied, the floor in the tiny outhouse had to be cleaned, but first the radio hidden there had to be taken out. So the job was usually done just before we listened to the news from

The alley next to the parsonage in Irnsum.

England. A suitcase full of documents was also hidden there, but later we took it to a safer place to divide the risk a bit.

Martien was so absentminded he would sometimes forget to put on his wooden shoes when he went out to get the milk can, even in the rain. That made things hard for me because he had only two pairs of socks, and one was always in the laundry. Both the laundry and bathing were problems. There were so many people to keep clean. On Friday evening the adults took baths, and on Saturday the kids did. The men and women bathed separately, but the children did it together.

Baths took a lot of time. In the washroom there was a huge pot of water that we first heated up with turf and wood. We sent the children to look for wood. For a while we used turf, but it was gone in no time.

Coal ships traveled along the Boorn, and I heard that every so often one of the ships stopped to exchange goods with the local people. But what did we have to exchange? Suddenly I remembered we had gotten a Christmas package from Douwe Egberts with shag tobacco that I could exchange. One afternoon a boy came by to say a new ship had arrived. We traded the tobacco for a few bags of coal, so we would have some heat for a while. The coal smoke turned everything brown and made the walls and ceilings look filthy, but that didn't bother me.

An and Herman in the garden of the parsonage in Irnsum.

An—Winter 1944-Spring 1945
Creative thinking and
the generosity of the country

*I*t wasn't only the fuel that worried me. The porridge we made for people who dropped in and were hungry was using up the wheat we had gotten for ourselves and that Clara used to make pancakes and even bread. We were all told to think about what we could give in exchange for these basic staples. I remember somebody saying, "I know, one of the children. We have got half a dozen of them. One less won't make a difference." He said it so seriously that we all scowled at him. I looked at the sweet little faces, and suddenly I had an idea. "You want to bet I can leave with two of Herman's books of sermons and come back with two bags of wheat?"

As soon as I said it, I realized I was being overly optimistic and almost lost my courage. But I had said it, so now I had to do my best. My idea meant riding a full day's bicycle trip all the way to Holwerd and another day's biking back home. The boys carefully attached Herman's bags to the back of my bike. I set out on the first dry day. It was cold in February, 1945, but that was not the worst of it. I asked Reverend Hoekema in Hallum if I could stay there overnight, and I was hospitably received. There was a cold wind from the north. I was exhausted and my back ached, but I had enough aspirins to make sure I got a good night's sleep.

The next day I got on my bike bright and early. As I approached the Biema farm, I felt my courage seeping away. I recognized the farm from the description I had been given. It was easy to find on a path down from the road. I waited next to a woman standing there with her bike, a child sitting on the back of it. She was having her bicycle bags filled by the friendly Frisian farmer who wished her a good trip. And then there I was. The man smiled and asked what I had to exchange, *"Sa jongfaam, wat hast do te ruljen?"* (So, little lady, what do you have to trade?) I couldn't say a word; I was tongue-tied.

A farm in Friesland.

The farmer picked up a cup, filled it from the barrel of wheat, and said, "First I'll fill your bag." The more cups of wheat he emptied into my bag, the more nervous I became. "Wait a minute," I said. I took the books of sermons and told him that was all I had. He looked at me as if he couldn't believe his eyes and said, "Where did you get those?" "They are my husband's sermons," I told him. "This is all we have to exchange." "I will fill your bags," he said. "How many of you are there at home?" "Usually eleven," I said, "but at night sometimes a lot more." He quietly looked at me and said, "Doesn't the church community take care of you?" I didn't know what to say.

He leaned my bicycle against the wall and led me inside where there was a wonderful aroma. One of the boys at the table pulled up an extra chair for me. The farmer introduced me as the preacher's wife from Irnsum, and fortunately he didn't say a word about what I had come to exchange. A kindhearted woman put a piece of meat on my dish and told me to help myself. After a delicious meal, he walked me back up to the road. I thanked him profusely, but all he said was, "God's word means more to me than a little bit of wheat. Have a safe trip home."

Something happened almost every day. Either someone was picked up, or there was a raid, or homes were searched. We saw Germans bicycling through our village, and usually their intentions were not good. Our house was on a bend in the road. One of the children noticed that German soldiers hid in the alley next to us where people came for food. Or because of the way the street lay, people would come upon the alley, unable to see the Germans who were standing in it. The Germans would stop them and not let them pass and take away what they had. Some of the children climbed carefully up on our roof and held up a big sign they had made—*"Turn around, there are Nazis here."* It worked. The Germans couldn't see them from where they were standing, and the people who had been warned hid somewhere and came back later.

For months, we hung posters on our windows saying we had diphtheria, just to keep the Germans away. The only one who got diphtheria though was Herman, and fortunately his was not a severe case. We were careful to make sure no one else got infected. No one could go into his room. I rinsed my hands with the Superol Dr. Smeding gave me.

I am still puzzled that with very few exceptions, we were never helped. As newlyweds, we didn't have a lot of supplies in the house and so we were able to exchange only a few things. We never asked anyone for anything. Later, when I was unable to get Farmer Pasma released, people said I had asked for a side of pork for my efforts. As I write this, I can still feel the pain of that accusation. No matter what good use we could have made of it, I never dreamed of asking for such a thing.

More and more truckloads of undernourished children were arriving. The situation in the west of the country was getting worse. In despair, parents sent their children away to what they hoped was a better place, not knowing if they'd ever see them again.

One hundred thousand Dutch people starved to death in the winter of 1944, called the Hunger Winter. Only women and old men, too old to be picked up and sent to the East Front as forced laborers, were free to find food. Most food was under control of the Nazis, who rationed it out in ever smaller daily bits. Women went on bicycles without rubber tires, since the rubber was all consigned for war use, riding on the wooden rims to farms outside the cities, hoping to get food. Mostly they got tulip bulbs or sugar beets. To keep warm, people burned tram rails and their wooden blocks in their stoves. Where houses were empty and the residents were unlikely to come back because they had been sent to concentration camps, the neighbors pulled out the support beams and burned them to keep warm. Public buildings not in use were also plundered in this struggle for survival.

The trucks carrying children arrived from the cities in the evening or at night. In the beginning it wasn't hard to find places for the children to stay, but soon it was more than just a few of them now and then. More trucks came and the groups got larger. One evening I was informed that a large group was coming, and that some of the children were sick. We prepared our attics for them with fresh hay and extra blankets. We were expecting them around midnight. I suppressed my emotions as much as I could when I saw the incredibly skinny children staring up at us with big frightened eyes, scared of the unknown. Right after they arrived, we got a call saying another group was on the way and would arrive around three in the morning. I spoke to the chairman of the evacuation committee about whether we could use an official location, the De Zee & Co. warehouse, which was nearby. Of course we could, he said. We went over there to see if everything was okay.

I had put the first group of about 30 children to sleep in the attic rooms when we heard the sound of engines just after three that morning. A huge truck with a much larger group of children was parked at the square, and it awakened the warehouse owner. Just as the chairman opened the door of the warehouse and started to help the children inside, the owner starting screaming about how he didn't know anything about this and how we had a lot of nerve, acting as if it was all right with him. When he caught sight of me, he was so enraged that he started shouting about how I was the last in a degenerate family line. The whole thing was so absurd that I burst out laughing and couldn't stop. But I continued bringing the children to the warehouse rooms where they would sleep. The man walked off, obviously embarrassed about his outburst, and never spoke to me again.

These children were in even worse shape than the first group of the night. I was afraid to give them anything but watery milk before they went to sleep. There was no room for any more children in the village. I

The Frisian landscape.

started asking at the farms and other villages in the vicinity. Hardly anyone said no.

In the morning, the people helping out at the infirmary washed all the children in our kitchen. Each child was given a dish of porridge made of more water than milk, so they wouldn't have trouble digesting it. Then we got them ready for the families who were going to take care of them. Lenze rang the village bell, and the families knew it was time to come pick up the new children. Usually the poor things were treated with tender loving care, but it happened sometimes that children were brought back to me a couple of days later because they wet the bed or did something else their host families didn't like. Those children usually stayed with us until they were feeling better, and then we would try again to send them on. We had barely any room for one more person at our house.

Resistance work in Friesland

*O*ur house kept filling up. After Martien and Rien and Clara, there came Piet Denys, Peter Wijers, and Lenze Meinsma, the son of the first painter at my family's ceramic factory. In Makkum, we had heard from Lenze's father that he was in trouble. He had been detained and then sent to dig tank embankments in Assen. He pretended to have stomach problems and went so far as to have his stomach pumped a couple of times. He claimed he was too weak to work and absolutely refused to. We informed Lenza that he was welcome at our home and that he should try and escape as soon as he could. On about January 10 we were told he had arrived somewhere in Akkrum. Could Herman please come and pick him up on his bike, because Lenza had to get past the guard who was always on duty on the bridge.

We thought up a sly trick. As soon as Herman arrived in Akkrum, he would call and let me know exactly how much time he had needed to get to the bridge. Then I would make sure I got to the bridge at exactly the right time and engage the guard in a conversation. I was already there when I saw Herman coming with Lenza on his bike, and I made sure the guard was standing with his back to them. I told the guard I wanted to continue our conversation, but I was cold and would prefer to stand in the sentry house. Speaking as loudly as I could, I tried to distract him, and it worked. We were in the middle of an animated conversation when I saw Herman and Lenza bicycle past. The wind also cooperated by making it almost impossible to hear them going by. Relieved, I was walking on air as I strolled back home. Lenze had to spend the first couple of days at our house recovering from everything he had been through and regaining his health.

Folkert was the first of the underground detainees to be brought home from prison in 1944. Then Boerlage managed to pass a message out of prison via a good guard, telling the Resistance that he no longer trusted himself not to break under questioning. He had held an important position in the regional Resistance. I was asked to go to Leeuwarden immediately to try to free him by making contact with Herr Gründmann, Head of the SS in Friesland.

I began by visiting with Gründmann about the congregation in Irnsum and telling him how difficult it was for us to help the members cope with the War. We talked about the wives whose husbands were off at work in Germany and who were left behind with too little food or fuel. The authority of the church was still respected, although I didn't think I would successfully persuade him to free Boerlage. Maybe because I knew so little about the particular Resistance group with which Boerlage was active, I wasn't nervous and could speak to Herr Gründmann in a relaxed way. (He was given the death penalty after the War ended.)

In time, my efforts paid off. After three trips by coach to Leeuwaarden, I got Boerlage's release papers and took them to the prison. My mission was to collect him and claim he was my cousin. One complication was that he didn't know me.

One of the prison guards was supposed to tell him what to expect. The guard had been described to me, but when I got to the office window, I didn't see him. I loudly pronounced the name of the man I was supposed to collect and the good guard stood right up. I was able to whisper to him that I was the man's "cousin." The guard went to get Boerlage. I hugged him warmly and said, "Hello cousin, I'm glad I was able to get you. There was a mistake."

Only when the coach was far outside Leeuwarden did he ask who I really was. Our meeting was socially uncomfortable, since he and Herman had had a major disagreement about church matters. Although he didn't like being rescued by his opponent's wife, that was totally unimportant compared to the fact that the whole regional organization had not been betrayed, which was the main concern!

An—Spring 1945
A pacifist's nightmare

One evening I was suddenly asked to take a message to the Resistance air base in Bozum, about 12 kilometers away. An arms ship docked right outside the village was going to be blown up the next day by English pilots. My message was that the Resistance was to tow the ship to Sneek Lake where it could be destroyed without doing any harm to the village. So I donned my nurse's uniform again and bicycled to Bozum.

It was inclement weather and very windy. I arrived at the farm and saw some men carrying things in heavy bags to a dung pile in a field in back of the house. There had been an unannounced arms dropping, and now there were not enough people to transport the weapons quickly to other locations. And there was no place to hide them at the base itself. (The guns were attached to a parachute and were supposed to be dropped out of an airplane at an agreed-upon spot at an agreed-upon time.)

This posed a problem for me. I had always said I would be willing to do anything but transport arms. That went against my conscience. But in this situation, I was in a dilemma. It was clear there was no way out of it. I would have to lay my principles aside and help with this immediate problem.

They tied a burlap bag around me and put in as many guns as would fit. I was wearing a wide jacket and could still close it. I delivered my message, and with a heavy feeling, literally and figuratively, I got on my bike again. Now the wind was at my back, but I still wasn't feeling good because I had broken my promise to myself. On my way, I wasn't even thinking about the Germans who might stop me. I was, after all, violating the curfew which ran from eight at night till six in the morning. A couple of kilometers before my destination, two Germans suddenly jumped out onto the road in front of me. They took me totally by surprise, but when I am scared I start cursing. Before I realized what I was doing I said, "You ought to be ashamed of yourselves! Scaring a pregnant woman like that. I have to get to the doctor right away. The baby is coming any minute." They took a look at the size of me and let me go. I should have taken the guns to Friens, but I was so upset, I bicycled straight home, tears streaming down my cheeks.

I threw the sack of guns under a bush in the garden and went to bed. I had totally forgotten in all the commotion that Herman wasn't home and that a woman I didn't know had come by late in the evening asking for a place to sleep. She was lying in Herman's place in the bed. We had no more beds and the hayloft was already housing two transports of children who had come that evening. Shivering with cold and misery, I warmed up against her. She immediately held me in her arms and comforted me without even asking the cause of my grief.

Years later we were in Bussum visiting an uncle of Herman's on his birthday. I barely knew his family. We didn't travel much, but we happened to be in the area that day. A lot of people had come by to wish the man a happy birthday. There was a big circle of people who all knew each other, and we were introduced to everyone. I chatted with the woman next to me, and she asked where we lived and how we were related to the host.

I noticed that a man sitting across the room kept staring at me. It made me uncomfortable, and when I caught his eye I asked him outright why he was staring at me like that. "It is so bizarre," he said. "In the spring of 1945 I slept in your husband's spot in your bed. I consoled you in the middle of the night when you burst into tears. You were cold and wet and I held you without saying a word. I was dressed as a woman and didn't know anything about you except I could spend the night at your home." It was such a strange coincidence. He had known at the time that I was also a Resistance courier and that something had gone wrong. You could hear a pin drop in the room; everyone was listening to our conversation. I walked over to him and said, "Thank you for consoling me." We hugged, both of us incredibly relieved that it was all over. I still cannot understand how this could have happened. Purely by chance? Not that I minded. This warmth that I feel inside when I think about it is a wonderful gift.

An—Spring 1945
When language became a give-away

I had been to Leeuwarden again to arrange to pick up Farmer Pasma, who had been arrested for possessing a radio. I convinced regional SS director Herr Gründmann that our village needed the farmer because he helped to supply our food. I planned to present Farmer Pasma's release papers at the prison the following day and bring him to Irnsum.

When I got home, I heard there had been a raid. The Germans had been at the house across the street, looking for the neighbors' son. They forced their way in and, although they didn't find him, they did find Rosie, a little Jewish girl sitting at the table. She dashed out and climbed up by way of a trap door into another neighbor's house. From there she ran out onto the street and into an alley with the Germans in hot pursuit. She fell into a ditch and they pulled her out. Muddy and dripping wet, they tossed her into a car. Her foster mother was already in the car. The Germans, disappointed about not finding who they were looking for, arrested three other men and took everybody to Sneek, where they put them all in one cell. Rosie was still muddy and wet, but they wouldn't let her change into clean clothes. They kept everyone there for two weeks, and then finally let them go. We weren't expecting that.

Because of the raid, and then the imprisonment of our visitors and villagers, I lost the good feeling about going to pick up Farmer Pasma the next day. When I learned that he had been sent out on one of the trains "by mistake," it was almost too much for me to take. Farmer Pasma was on the train and little Rosie had been picked up—we didn't expect to ever see either of them again.

Despite all of that, another truck filled with children arrived that night. Marijke, who was staying with the Meinsmas, had been so frightened by the Germans picking up Rosie that we had to find some other arrangement for her. I suggested adding her to the new group and finding a foster family for her as one of the "hungry children" the next day. She spent that night at our house, sleeping with her mother again. In itself, that made it a very special occasion. That night I picked up an ID card with a picture of a child with dark curls, whom I thought looked enough like Marijke to pass. I copied the other girl's information on a card and put it on a string around her neck.

At breakfast, Marijke sat at the head of the table with Clara on her right and me on her left so she wouldn't have any direct contact with the other children. They weren't supposed to know that she already spoke Frisian, our local dialect, which none of the newly arrived hungry children would have yet learned. Suddenly something happened that disconcerted the children and us, too. Marijke climbed up on her chair and said in perfect Frisian, "There is Uncle Fritz!" Everyone looked up, but none of the children knew what she was talking about. They were a motley crew, loaded onto the trucks by parents in despair, who just hoped they would come home someday safe and sound. The children didn't even know each other. Uncle Fritz was the old boatsman Marijke would see sail down the Boorn every morning. She had been hiding in that little upstairs room for a year and a half. He always waved at her and she waved back. He had no idea she was a *Judenkind*. The moment she spoke the words, she realized what she had said. She looked at us in anguish, but we pretended not to notice.

When we had all the children registered and examined, Lenze the town crier went through the village with the bell, and the families came, each to pick up one or more children. Including Marijke. Wim Meinsma was there, too. When it was Marijke's turn, she stood there with her bulging suitcase and I heard someone say, "You see, that pretty girl is going to one of those Mennonite families, that is the way it is." But when the Liberation finally came and the Meinsmas took their seats in the empty window of their store, openly appearing with Marijke and her mother, our Clara, everyone then understood the real relationship between the "pretty child" and Clara, and why we had hidden both of them in plain sight, across the street from each other. I happened to be standing there when this same woman walked past the shop window. She looked at me without saying a word. She was obviously embarrassed. "That is the way it was," I said.

Lynn with one of the quilts.

Lynn—1988
Still tender hearts

*I*n 1988, I discovered a Twinning Project between the Mennonite Peace Group and a network called Israelis and Palestinians for Nonviolent Solutions. The Project came from the heart of my marriage and from my deepest wish for peace for my husband and my Jewish friends. I joined immediately. Soon thereafter, several Israelis and Palestinians for Nonviolent Solutions came to the Netherlands. They rarely saw each other except for hour-long meetings after difficult travel through roadblocks. They wanted to get to know each other more personally so they could do more effective work when they returned to Israel/Palestine. And they wanted to get to know their Dutch partners.

Three Palestinians and two Israelis came for a weekend conference and tour. Chaya Beckerman, one of the Jewish delegates, stayed at our house overnight. She was originally from Minneapolis, the state I come from, and was now actively involved in bringing busloads of Israelis to a peace center to meet with their Palestinian neighbors. Her stay with us was spontaneous—and I had already scheduled a trip to Friesland the following morning to collect the quilts from An's house for our store's Thanksgiving display. I asked Chaya to join me for the ride.

Without telling An that I would not be coming alone, we drove through the Frisian countryside on a gorgeous, sunny morning, remarking about how much the landscape reminded us of Minnesota. We arrived at the farmhouse where I had first seen the quilts, driving up over a narrow brick road obviously not made for cars. We got out, went to the farmhouse door, and knocked. A man answered and, ignoring me, addressed Chaya. "Are you Roosje?" he asked, a tremor in his voice. "No, I'm Chaya," she answered. "Nice to meet you."

"But you're from America?" he asked.

"Yes," she said, "from Minnesota originally. Now I live in Israel."

An and Herman

"But you don't know this place? You haven't been here before?"

"No," she answered. "Lynn just brought me along to keep her company on the ride."

With that he invited us into the living room of the still-picturesque farmhouse. His wife served us strong coffee and Friese spicecake with orange frosting. The couple, Herman and An Keuning, were visibly shaken by Chaya's presence. I thought perhaps I had crossed an etiquette line by bringing another person with me unannounced. But I didn't risk asking because I didn't want to insult Chaya.

We admired the quilts. An told Chaya the story of how they had come into her care; I told the story of how I had happened upon the farmhouse with the quilts inside. Then An and Herman explained why they had been so shocked to see Chaya, whom they thought was Roosje.

Roosje was one of nine Jewish children hidden in the small village from the Nazis during the occupation of Holland. None of the residents of the town ever talked with each other about the children, even though one childless couple had suddenly sprouted a four-year-old! The Dutch villagers couldn't be sure whom to trust. For the duration of the war, all went well, until the week just before the Liberation when someone ratted on the presence of the children. The SS came into the village, rounded them up, and carried them off for execution. All except Roosje. A teenager, she made a run for it, diving into a canal to hide. A soldier shot into the water, hitting her. She was also carried off, but to a hospital. A week later, the hospital was liberated, and Roosje was allowed to go to California to be raised further by family there. The entire village never saw their beloved Roosje again after her desperate dive into the water.

Nine-Patch (denim)

When Chaya appeared at An and Herman's door some 40 years later, they thought that because I was an American, I had brought Roosje back for a visit.

Although it was Chaya who appeared, and not Roosje, An began telling me stories from the Underground. Fascinated, I asked An to write them down. We've been working on this project ever since at a very slow pace.

Herman with Butschalowsky's Bible and personal note.

An—1945
Classic diversion

Clara, the Jewish fugitive who lived with us, was often anxious because of all the people who were constantly walking in and out of our house. We felt it preferable that our pastor's assistants have freedom of movement in the house and garden; no one understood who they were or how many of them there were anyway. The German officer quartered with the van der Goot family didn't even know. He was responsible for all the waterway transport between Lemmer and Groningen. Irnsum is on the Boorn River, which is part of this waterway.

The officer imagined himself a welcome guest at the parsonage, an attitude we used to our advantage. I managed to get on his good side after he mentioned that he could issue passes over the Ijssel Bridge for anyone who needed to cross over in certain situations. He welcomed my interest in the passes, and once let me see them. He told me that if you had one of his passes you could walk over the bridge without any further check. Those passes would certainly come in handy. I knew where he kept them in his desk drawer, and I helped myself whenever we needed to give them to refugees who had to go back over the Ijssel Bridge.

There was a whole pile of them that needed his stamp. I visited the officer weekly. Herman would call after I had been there for a while to say it was time for dinner. The telephone was on the wall in the hallway. I heard Herr Butschalowsky say that I should be able to be home in about 10 minutes. While he was on the phone, I had time to stamp the passes and sit down again with a pile of them now inside my blouse. During another visit, I asked him to please turn the portrait of Hitler around because I couldn't stand the look in his eyes. He recklessly did as I asked.

This "friendship" was a big help to lots of the people who came to us looking for food. I don't remember exactly how many passes I stuffed

A bridge on the outskirts of Irnsum.

into my blouse. We heard afterwards that the passes were also useful at other checkpoints. During one of my chats with Butschalowsky, I explained why our house was always so full of the young men who aroused his curiosity. Herman had a large working territory so he needed a lot of pastor's assistants. The officer later even offered them a house where they all could stay!

I told Butschalowsky that we sat together every evening between eight and nine to talk about the day and invited him to join us, knowing that the SD (*Sicherheids Dienst* or German security police, a division of the dreaded SS headed by Himmler) in Grouw could invade at any moment while on their routine patrol in Irnsum. If their officer were with us, we would be covered. So Officer Butschalowsky was our frequent guest. I always sat between him and Clara. One evening he suddenly said, "You can always tell if you are sitting among Aryans—it feels so good." I felt Clara stiffen, so I went around with the teapot again, and then asked Clara to put another kettle on to heat in the kitchen and also to fetch the paper. She disappeared safely, but she didn't dare return.

Butschalowsky was a Nazi and had to pay for his behavior later, even though he did nothing really evil. He came to see us once after the War. I found it a difficult visit, because I felt so guilty about betraying his trust. So I told him straight off where we stood during the War and that we had needed him; in fact, we had used him. Although shocked by my revelation, he wanted to keep in contact with us. He felt so guilty about his role in the War that he was grateful to me for having duped him. "At least," he said, "my presence in Irnsum, thanks to you, was not all bad!"

It was not until 1974 that I had the courage to accept his repeated invitations to come to his home, and then only under exceptional circumstances. The flags of Friesland and the Netherlands hung from the doorjamb of his house when we arrived. He addressed us formally at dinner, saying, "Finally now there is peace for me!" I felt ashamed. He had had his punishment long before then, and I had added to it. We kept in touch, and before he died he gave Herman the Bible he had with him in Irnsum. He had written, "Thank you for the friendship" and a lengthy note to us and taped it inside his Bible. By then, our friendship had become real.

After spending a year in prison, Hans Butschalowsky wrote to the Jewish Council, offering to take in and raise two Jewish orphans as his way of making recompense. He was saddened when his offer was refused, even after we explained to him that all the Jewish orphans were being sent to Israel to be raised there, and that none of them were being placed in any European or American homes.

An

An—1945
Saved by the dead

One day an important figure in the regional Resistance was caught. So our neighbor across the yard, a member of the group, disappeared into the night. After chartering a flat-bottomed boat, he loaded his possessions and set off into hiding somewhere on the Boorn River. The next morning I happened to be giving the upstairs bedroom a thorough cleaning. Shaking out a rug, I saw to my horror that the familiar wicker briefcase, which held all the documents about the regional underground network, had been left behind in the middle of this man's otherwise empty living room!

I ran downstairs, across the road, grabbed a small metal saw out of another neighbor's work shed, and tried to saw through one of the iron bars on a basement window. A passerby helped me. I had the thinnest child with me and he just managed to squeeze through the slats. He grabbed the briefcase, wriggled it through the window, and came back home with it. And just in time—in the distance I saw the Greens (German security police, who wore green uniforms) approaching.

But now where to hide the briefcase? It was certain that our house would soon be searched! I took the case quickly through the backyard to the neighbor's yard, where I knew three young men were hiding in a hollow under a turf pile. I left it with them, thinking it was secure there. But that evening, the neighbor showed up at my back door with the briefcase; the boys hadn't dared to keep it. They were dodging the Nazi forced labor conscription of all Dutch males between the ages of 18 and 45.

What now? I had to find a place to hide the case, and I had to find it fast. I decided to carry out the plan I had thought up earlier. There was a woman who had just passed away lying in state in our rear living room. She had an enormous hunchback. I called Clara to help me decide whether it was a good idea. Together we managed to hide the suitcase in the hollow of her back. We

A house behind the parsonage's back garden in Irnsum.

put an extra blanket over her so if anyone searched the house, they wouldn't find anything.

Just as a precaution, all the men and older boys went to stay somewhere else, and Clara went to the Meinsma family. But I hadn't been left behind all alone; the girls who helped on night duty were still there, and other children were in the study. Besides that, we had a couple of refugees in the front room. Our house had a number of more or less permanent residents, in addition to the refugees who were on the run and Resistance people on a special mission who would stay for a night or two.

That night I sensed there was going to be a raid and I was well prepared. I had put a notice on the "infirmary" door that said "Diphtheria." When the doorbell rang, I opened the door in a state of tranquility. Two *Grüne Polizei* (Green Police) stood there, and they immediately marched inside. I opened the door to the "infirmary," and they took a step back when they saw the patients. They ran up the stairs to where the children were already fast asleep, only to waken them and have them start crying in unison. The *Polizei* banged their rifles against the walls in the closets and ceilings, asked me why there was hay on the floor in the attic, and then went downstairs again.

They asked me where *Herr Pfarrer* was (*Pfarrer* means minister). I told them Herman was somewhere else for his work and hadn't been able to make it back before the eight o'clock curfew. They searched the kitchen and pantry downstairs. I hoped they would skip the rear living room, especially since at first they walked past it on the way to the cellar. I decided to open the door though. The oldest police officer was surprised to see me suddenly do that; he looked at me as if he thought I was trying to trick him. When he pulled the sheet off the casket, he saw the serene face of a little old lady. He pulled the sheet down further. I could see the corner of the wicker basket sticking out, so I just walked around the casket and straightened out the sheet. The other man could see just as much as I could, but they left it at that, and, after a few warnings and remarks about how they had had their fill of all these refugees and patients, they were gone.

The night guards came rushing up to me. The girls who helped me during the night with caring for the patients knew what could have happened. In the beginning, no one knew the purpose poor dead Mrs. Honcoop had served. The men came back to the house, and Herman came home and picked up the Bible, which I had demonstratively opened on the table, and started reading. At his request, we all sat down and listened. If you open the Bible at random, it will often open at the Psalms, as was now the case. Herman started to read from Psalm 31. I slowly felt my tension dissolve and the cold feeling inside me leave. All of us were aware of the danger we had just sidestepped. Herman closed the reading with a prayer. We went back to our places. I walked through the house with a sense of gratitude. And I gave a special thank you to Mrs. Honcoop.

This was one of those moments when I realized I was responsible for all these patients, men and boys, refugees and Resistance fighters on their way to a job, Jews, and children, all of whom more or less permanently lived here. I knew anything could happen, but I still felt that I was doing what I was supposed to be doing. I had to go on. This was what I was given to do. Maybe things would be totally different tomorrow. Maybe new jobs would await me. I did not have any trouble sleeping at night, because I had faith and trust that this was my life to live.

An—1945
Coincidence?

*A*nd then the stream of evacuees stopped. But just when we thought the front and rear rooms downstairs would be empty and that we would have our living room again, the space was requisitioned as an emergency infirmary by the Germans. A German-speaking medical officer came in with three medics, and they started converting the rooms. We realized that the Front was getting closer. An Allied parachute invasion was expected in the area around Leeuwarden, and so the medics were preparing for numerous casualties on the German side.

The first evening at dinner-time after this new use of our home, we were sitting at the table in the crowded dining room, the remaining children at their own separate table, about to share bread. Bread is all we had. There was a knock at the door. The medical officer came in and asked permission to use our stove to fry an egg. With his own frying pan, a chunk of bacon, and two eggs in his hand, he got busy. In no time, the room filled with a delicious, almost-forgotten aroma. No one said a word.

The man felt the quiet and looked up to see us all watching him, mesmerized. He stood straight up, pulled out his pistol, and turned a full circle. He saw our surprised and frightened faces, screamed, and dashed out of the room. We heard him crying in the hall. I went out to him. He was crouching in the corner behind the door, crying his eyes out. He looked up at me, distraught and at his wits' end. Before he knew what was happening, I had my arms around him. He was just a boy in his early twenties, barely older than me.

In jerks he managed to tell me what was so wrong. He was a Polish German, and during a raid he had been given a choice: join the army or get a bullet in his head. It was a hard decision for him and his medics. They were all Mennonites who believed in nonviolence. But with the permission of the Mennonite elders, the young men went with the army to Russia. This officer had just finished studying medicine, so it was his job to work with the medics and care for the ill and wounded. That initially gave him less of a sense of guilt, because he wasn't expected to participate directly in the violence of war (although he clearly carried a pistol for self-protection).

But in the hell that Russia was in those days, he discovered that whenever it got very quiet around him, it was wise to fear for his life. That was what happened in our room, and when he saw only innocent, frightened faces, something snapped inside him. He saw his home in us, his village. "We are Mennonites and have promised God not to kill," he said. We looked at each other. I thought it was safe to tell him he had come to a Mennonite parish. "Unbelievable," was the only word he could utter. Deeply moved, we sat there together. He called over his medics. We went back into the room where the fried eggs were now shriveled up on the corner of the stove. The children still thought they were a great delicacy though, and each took a bite.

We held a service of gratitude that evening with all the residents, including the medics who participated fully. I can still remember the singing and feel the fellowship and joy surrounding this "coincidence."

An—March 1945
Collaborators try to flee

*O*ne more group of children came to us during those last weeks
of the War in March, 1945. One morning the village policeman
asked me to go with him to a ship docked behind the old dairy factory. The people who lived nearby told him they heard the sound of children crying. He thought it was suspicious, so we walked over there
together. He opened one of the ship's shutters, and there was a horrible
smell. We saw a hull filled with children lying in the hay, barely moving.
They were crying softly and whimpering, a very sad sight. We asked them
where the people taking care of them were, and a few said, "In the cabin."
When we opened the door to the cabin, we were met by a different smell.
In a drunken stupor, a couple of men were lying there, unable to utter a
single coherent sentence.

We ran for help. I went home and got the German-speaking medical
officer and his medics. They helped us examine the children. A few needed medical care and were taken to the hospital. We took four or five children home. The doctor didn't think they would survive if he didn't go to
the Front for new medicine. Lenze went into town with the bell and, once
again, we found temporary homes for all the children. It was a great relief.
Especially the Catholic families, which were often already large, opened
their doors. What an exhausting day.

With a great deal of tender loving care, the "boys" nursed the children.
The next day Hans, the Mennonite medical officer, went to the Front on
his motorcycle. He had to cross the Rhine to get penicillin. Despite the
danger it put him in, he managed to do the job. He never told us how. All
the children recovered, though it did take a couple of weeks. By that time,
the medics were long gone.

The ship the children had come on was from The Hague. It had been
commandeered by NSBers, Dutchmen who collaborated with the Nazis

and were now trying to get away. The ship was full of kids whose parents had put them on board, fearing desperately for their lives. Tens of thousands of people were dying. There was no food in the cities. Without even a list of the names of the children, nor their return addresses, the ship sailed out but lost its captain on the way. Some of the children might have been of NSB parents, who wanted to avoid having their stigma pass on to their children.

The village policeman turned the NSBers over to the Domestic Forces in the Netherlands, an organization of Resistance groups established in 1944.

There were three collaborators (*Landwacht*) in our village who had been influenced by the barber, who was sympathetic to the Germans. There was also a member of the SS, who was so bitter about his own plight that he was a very dangerous man. When it looked like the Liberation was coming in September, 1944, he was afraid of *bijltjesdag* or hatchet day, the day the rest of the country would take revenge on the Dutchmen who had sided with the Germans. He expressed his fears to our verger Jan Dijkstra. The man told Dijkstra he realized he had bet on the wrong horse. He assumed it would be an eye for an eye, and asked Dijkstra for help.

That is when Dijkstra came to us. We promised the man he could come to us if he sensed any danger, but he would not be able to escape his proper punishment. Herman would personally hand him over. When he came to our back door one Saturday evening, I saw a man who slithered up to the attic to sleep in the hay like a frightened little boy. I told him not to go outside, but when we got home from church the next day, he was gone. He had fled out the back door into the fields, a very foolish thing to do.

By then the Domestic Forces in the Netherlands had become active. Since the Queen and Cabinet were still in England and local authority had been taken over by the German occupiers, an informal organization of Resistance workers had set up an alternative defense and civil order system. The Domestic Forces were armed as they patrolled the streets and fetched members of the *Landwacht* (collaborators) from their homes. They didn't find this particular SS officer in our home, but after he fled into the fields, it wasn't long before they caught him. Someone spotted him the very next morning.

Soon thereafter, the Canadians came through and liberated our town. People stood around on the street talking to get some of the tension out of their system. Suddenly we heard cheering and laughing from the distance, and we soon saw what was going on. Guns slung over their shoulders, a couple of guys from the new Domestic Forces were leading the way, followed by the SS man who was being frog-marched by the hostile crowd.

I called Herman who had gone inside, exhausted from all the emotions. "Come here, this is wrong." Without a moment's hesitation, he jumped off the curb into the procession and frog-marched alongside the prisoner voluntarily. A heavy silence came over the street. The guys from the Domestic Forces stopped in their tracks. Herman said, "Do not do anything you will be ashamed of later. Do not repay evil with evil." Slowly, the villagers turned around and went home. The Domestic Forces continued walking through town with the man between them, clearly humiliated. He was soon handed over to the authorities for his proper punishment.

Now we could see how many people had been hiding in the village and on the farms in the vicinity. The village was crowded that evening. It was lovely weather. It was so good to see each other—there was such an intense

joy—but mixed in was fear for our relatives and friends who had not yet returned. I still know exactly how I felt—shaky and uncertain about the troops I had been cheering on, who were now supposed to bring about total peace. I couldn't take my eyes off the people in our house. The sick children and the healthy ones, the refugees and the folks in hiding, liberated now from their fears and cares but still concerned about people for whom this was not yet the case. We were all aware of that, and our evening prayers were filled with gratitude and our hope for peace.

Herman

That evening, Herman visited the wives of the six collaborators who had been arrested. They were very glad to see him. He consoled them and encouraged them and told them they were still part of the community.

The next day, the Domestic Forces took over our living room. They stood on our stoop with the biggest rifles around. I asked them to please put the guns somewhere else, but they said they couldn't do that; they had to clean them. So we took the sick children upstairs again. They didn't like that one bit. They liked being with the people downstairs and being visited by the other children from their group who would come by now and then.

We were nervous about the Forces parading through the village with rifles and wondered if there weren't going to be accidents. Our fears turned out to be justified. One morning, the men were sitting around polishing their rifles. One of them thought the magazine was empty and pulled the trigger. A shot was fired. We were all scared for a minute, but no one was wounded. When I saw where the bullet went through the ceiling, I thought my heart had stopped. The girls were upstairs, and their beds were just about where the bullet had gone. I rushed up to see. I didn't hear a sound from the girls' room. With big frightened eyes, they were lying in the double bed. A miracle had happened! The bullet had gone right between them and wound up in a ceiling beam. I couldn't stop shivering as I embraced them and took them downstairs to our bed. They were scared silly. Fortunately nothing else bad happened, but from then on the Domestic Forces in the house were more careful.

An with a Makkum dinner plate.

My father and mother helped the Underground from the very start of the Occupation as an expression of their moral resistance to Nazism. When all the people of Makkum were told to evacuate for their own safety just before the German invasion, my parents decided that our family would stay put. My father, Jan Pieter Tichelaar, was a city councilman and a patriarch of the town, and he also wanted to protect our century-old family factory. (Begun in 1559, the factory is the oldest family business operating in the Netherlands today.)

At the very end of the War, the German SSers came to Makkum. Although not a single underground fugitive, including Jews, had been betrayed during the War, a tragic event now occurred. One of the Resistance workers got caught, the others were betrayed, and all of them were rounded up and executed. My father was able to escape this fate because the servant girl saw what was happening on her way to work. Although her brother was a minor helper in the Resistance, she was more concerned with my father, who played a major role. So she went on to work and rousted her employer out of bed. He went out the window to his hiding place until the roundup was over. The girl's own brother was not so fortunate. He lost his life as an underground hero.

Irnsum was liberated before Makkum. On the day Makkum was liberated, I went back to my hometown as a passenger in the car that belonged to the notary from Roordahuizen. He had dug it out from under the hay where he had hidden it during the War. Accompanied by two Domestic Forces guys who had been granted permission by their commander to make the trip, I caught a ride home to Makkum. At De Meer, we couldn't drive any farther because there was still shooting going on. So I hitched a ride for the rest of the way in a jeep with the first Canadian liberators. By now the shooting had stopped and a white flag was flying high. But there had just been an attack on the lane leading into the village.

I saw the corpses of soldiers lying in a hole. Farther down, on the corner of Bleekstraat, were more dead bodies. There was rubble all over and the remains of wiring. I will never forget the craters in the streets of Makkum, the sizzling electric cables snaking over the ground, and my father, standing tall at the city square to greet the Canadians. I jumped out of the jeep and ran over to him. He couldn't believe his eyes. "What are you doing here?" were the first words out of his mouth. Then he saw the smiling Canadians in the jeep. They promised to come pick me up later. Near my family's house we saw Kornstra's houseboat, half sunk. It had been hit by shells, which sent the gravel that covered the roof flying all over, making holes in the windows and doors.

I walked home where my mother was preparing a tiny dinner with the good dishes for the first time in ages. She went to fetch a milk jug from the glass cabinet. The cabinet was whole except for one little hole. Our house, next to the factory, stood on a canal. A piece of gravel from Kornstra's boat had flown into the cabinet and taken the ear off the milk jug, a curious sight. Mother stood there holding it, surprised, and then she saw me. We are not the kind of family to make a show of our emotions, but that day we connected, heart to heart without any holding back.

Our house was still in pretty good shape. Everyone had stayed safe in the cellar. Some people in the town had died, and the village was in ruins, but we were free! I remember the jeep beeping the horn on the dike, signaling it was time to leave, much too soon. Happy and grateful, I climbed in to drive back with them. Everyone standing around the jeep waved good-bye to us. Back in Irnsum, relaxed and with a heavy weight lifted from my shoulders, I realized how fortunate I was that all my relatives and friends were still alive.

Makkum dinnerware in An and Herman's retirement home.

Herman and An

An—May 1945
After the Liberation

When the War officially ended on May 5, 1945, the Domestic Forces disappeared from our living room. This event was followed by a thorough housecleaning. The first thing we did was remove the hay from the attic rooms. A lot of people came to help transform the house into a clean and inviting open parish, just the way I wanted it. In the rear room with its wall-to-wall rug, we even managed to get the floor totally clean. Piet Meinsma turned the twisted mats in the study. The house was ours again! The guests gradually disappeared. Many of them had lost their families or were unsure where to go. In fact, the last one didn't leave until September, 1945.

I escorted the children all the way to Amsterdam, a beautiful experience. Trucks took them to the meeting point in Lemmer, where there were ships waiting to take them over the Ijsselmeer to Amsterdam. I can still remember how, late at night, with the children asleep in the hull, we carried the toilet barrels up the stairs and tossed the contents overboard. It was a quiet night, thankfully, and the children didn't get seasick. I don't recall how many ships there were, or exactly how many different places the children were from, to which they would return. But I do remember the convoy of army trucks behind the Central Station, ready to take the children farther.

I went on the truck that carried most of the children I knew, and we took each of them to their homes. That was a very moving experience. I was about to collapse when I stood at the Central Station waiting for the boat to take me back home. I could not stop the tears streaming down my cheeks. I had seen so much, and I felt small and grateful that we had been able to help so many people relieve their misery. I have no idea how I got back home. I could just see the faces of the mothers. That's when I began to understand what it had meant to them to have to send their children away. I saw joy on their faces, and gratitude, and traces of guilt as they smothered their children with kisses.

I also don't know how the four sick children from The Hague got home later when they were strong enough to travel. It wasn't until the War was over that we were able to get information about how to contact their parents.

And then, after everyone left, Herman and I were in the house together, just the two of us. It was strange, after such a draining year, with so much happening and barely a moment together. All we had done was work side by side. But now we had time to sit down and think about what we wanted to do next. Should we just go on? Our whole relationship had always been based on what we were doing and that was good, but I wanted more. I wanted to show Herman more of who I was inside, and I wanted to get to know him better. This had not really been a good way to start a marriage. And now I was afraid Herman might be disappointed in me because of my back problems.

I had not gone again to see the neurologist who said he could find nothing wrong with my back. Even though my backaches were getting worse, I didn't think it would be helpful to return to him. I did start to have fainting spells more often. But they were short, so we didn't pay too much attention to them. The important thing was for me to be able to sit on the right kind of chair.

In August, 1945, Tom Smeding had a reception at his home to celebrate having been a physician for 25 years. Among his guests were some of his fellow doctors. During the evening I happened to be face to face with the very neurologist I had once been to see. It gave me such a fright that I fainted at his feet. He helped me up and said, "You never came back. I am expecting you later this week." I went back to see him, and he informed me that I was not psychologically mature yet, that I was having hysterical fits just to attract attention.

I felt like he had branded me, that I was nothing, nobody. But I thought it odd that I had been able to cope with all the things that had occurred during the years just past. Herman simply assumed that since he was the doctor, he had to be right. But still, the things this doctor said did not ring true to me.

I made an appointment for an examination with a different doctor in Heerenveen later that year. I would have a special liquid injected into my spine so the doctor could see if there was blockage anywhere. I had the injection on Saturday morning; then I had to stay in the hospital the whole weekend, sitting without moving so the liquid could move down my spine. On Monday they would x-ray my back to see if I was crazy, or if there was something physically wrong. Sunday evening I had visitors, and it was very pleasant. But I gradually started to see everything upside down. I was nauseous, and then it got worse. Finally I had to ask the visitors to leave. I was afraid to open my eyes. A young nurse in the bed next to mine saw that I wasn't feeling well and tried to lift my spirits. We would have the results on Monday. It was a long, horrible weekend.

Monday morning the senior nurse came by to say that the woman next to me could go home. I had the curtain around my bed closed to make my world as small as possible. She opened the curtain, took one look at me, and dashed off to get the neurologist. Now it is going to happen, I thought. They are going to take me for the X-rays. But, no, they just made a big commotion. They all seemed nervous. I had to lie on my side so they could give me a lumbar puncture. For three days, they gave me a handful of sulphur tablets twice a day and told me to drink a lot of water. I felt so sick.

Monday evening, they talked about maybe calling Herman to come. He had not been to see me because he was at a preachers' conference in Amsterdam. When he came on Tuesday, they told him the examination had been stopped because I had not responded well. It was not until later that we heard I had meningitis. The enormous amount of sulphur they gave me caused inflammation all through my body, including in my stomach, liver, and mucous membranes. Medical students from Groningen came in to look at me. I was bright yellow, my urine was like muddy coffee, and my bowel movements were like putty. Three weeks later, they sent me home. I had lost about a third of my normal weight.

Herman and my mother were called in to see the doctor, who told them that they had found nothing, that I simply had a tendency towards hysteria. He told them not to mention my back again and I would gradually get over it. I was left out of the conversation altogether. For 14 years, I felt negated. I had to do my best just to feel as though I belonged.

A group of the Russian Mennonite refugees who were sheltered in Irnsum.
Herman and An are in the center of the back row.

An—Late 1945-September 1946
More refugees?

In late 1945, a group of about 400 Mennonites from the Ukraine reached the Dutch border after a treacherous flight out of their country on the heels of Hitler's army. Rev. Hylkema discovered them hiding and miserable in the vicinity of Gronau, on the German side of the border with Holland. We were asked through a request in our Sunday paper to take them into our homes for a year. By then arrangements would be completed for their emigration to Paraguay, where they would join other refugee colonies. In Irnsum and the surrounding villages, Herman was in charge of finding homes for 50 of them. I was very happy, because here were people who didn't know anything about me. We volunteered to have two of them stay at our home.

The group arrived at the church on January 4, 1946, and from there the hosts were to take them home. Most of these refugees were women and young children, since the men and children above the age of 14 had been exiled to Siberia by the Russian communist authorities. Just having a Bible in your possession was enough reason to be arrested. These people had been roaming for more than two years before they came to us. They had

Makkum dinnerware

clearly been through very hard times and looked far older than they were. I saw members of our Mennonite congregation look at the group in a calculating way, and I didn't like it. No one had been assigned to any family yet, so I tried to divide up the group as well as I could. There were two more people than on the list, so we ourselves took four guests—the Bräuel family: a father, a mother, and two daughters.

The food for the refugees came from Food for Relief by way of MCC (Mennonite Central Committee, a North American Mennonite relief agency). Their Dutch office was in Amsterdam, and the food was distributed throughout Holland in vans. There was no additional money available to defray the costs of the refugees. Not knowing any better, the refugees ate off the extremely valuable decorative Makkumer pottery I had bought from our family's factory. I didn't know what to do about it, and I didn't want to embarrass our guests, so I mentioned my dilemma to Rev. Hylkema on his next visit. "Oh, that's no problem," he exclaimed. "There's a hat I've been eyeing on your hat rack for some time. It fits me just perfectly. Give me the hat and I'll get you 24 place settings." And he did!

Another problem was that we had happily burned all the vermin-infested bedding following the Liberation when the last guest left our house in September, 1945. We had no mattresses left for the Russian refugees. None of our neighbors had anything to lend us either. I called the Mennonite Central Committee to ask for help. "No problem," they said, and the next day a van arrived with a pile of quilts. Unfamiliar with the word "quilt," we were expecting blankets and were disappointed with these thin cotton things. Especially the older folks were very cold at night. So I called MCC again, begging for mattresses and blankets. Once again, no luck. "But," said Mr. Dyck, "we've got lots and lots and lots of quilts here. Why don't I send you enough to stuff into a mattress cover so the people can sleep ON them?" Some 50 handmade quilts arrived, enough to layer into mattress casings with top covers to spare. With another blanket borrowed from Piet and Wim Meinsma, we were fine.

Every evening, the whole group of 21 Ukrainian Mennonites staying in Irnsum gathered in our front room to sing, drink tea, and have evening services. Herman always closed the evening with a Bible text. I had furnished nearly the whole front room with old church seats. From the start,

I was touched by the way these people sang with all their souls. Consolation, pain, and sadness were in their voices. They sang to rise above it all and to face an uncertain future. When I sat with them, as I often did, and listened to their stories, I sometimes felt ashamed. Some of them were being treated badly at the homes where they were staying, even though they were with Mennonite families. I couldn't understand how that could happen; I didn't know what to say. Nor did I have the courage to do anything about it. The only thing I did was go to the homes and ask how everything was going, if there were any problems, if they were having trouble with anyone. The result was that we soon had two more women at our home. One was not in good health (she had turned out not to be of much use to the family she was staying with), and the other had to mop up the cellar every day because of a leak. And that was at the home of a carpenter! The former, Greta Andres, was a very sweet person who could spin and sew beautifully.

The Bräuels were the only married couple in the group. Their daughters worked at the sewing room of De Zee & Co. Fräulein Wiebe, who had been staying somewhere else at first, was a pianist. She was the daughter of one of the czar's physicians. After the Revolution, she went into hiding for 23 years in the countryside and worked as a midwife to make a living. No wonder she put on airs at our house, but it did cause quite a bit of irritation. Whenever she broke anything, she promised to pay for it "as soon as I regain my rightful standing." We never heard from her again. She certainly did not act or look anything like the others.

The refugees slept in the attic with their beds in hospital formation. We used the single bedstead downstairs as a bathing room because you could close the bedstead doors for privacy. We conversed in a mixture of Fries dialect, German, and *Plautdietsch*, the dialect spoken by those Mennonites who had migrated from Holland into Russia many years before. Greta Andres spent many days at our house hunched over the spinning wheel. She had a bad back, but she made a tablecloth of wheat flour sacks.

Mr. and Mrs. Bräuel looked like they were in their seventies, exhausted and gray-haired before their time because of what they had been through. Mr. Bräuel was in poor health and had a cough that didn't sound good. Their daughters, Marga and Nelly, said they had all been examined at the border in Enschede and there was nothing wrong with any of them.

Quilts come to An

The supplies which MCC distributed had come to Holland from North American Mennonites, mainly through the port of Rotterdam. An and Herman first asked for food for seven people since they did not have ration coupons for themselves either. Then they asked the MCC office for blankets and mattresses, but received only thin quilts, which they were unacquainted with. The Dutch usually slept under woolen blankets made locally, or under feather-filled duvets. When An and Herman made a second urgent request for bedding, they received about 40 more quilts and comforters for their household. As far as An can recall, their home was the only household needing new bedding, since their house had been used as a transit stop for hundreds of vermin-infested evacuees during the war. Marie Brunk, who supervised the MCC relief goods depot in Amsterdam, handed the quilts to An—first very thin ones, and on a second trip, thicker ones (comforters) which they could bind together and use as mattresses.

An recalls that the Russian émigrés were able to leave for Paraguay in early 1947. They were given fresh quilts and clothing on the ship. The quilts they had used in Friesland stayed behind with An and Herman. Some were worn out, some were given to bazaars or used as fundraising objects, and the rest she kept in memory of the War years and their aftermath. They were all heavily worn.

I had my doubts though, as Mr. Bräuel moved more slowly, lost weight, and spent a lot of time upstairs. I could hear him coughing a lot, too. I consulted Dr. Smeding who came to have a look at him. He concluded that Mr. Bräuel was suffering from severe strain and a bad cold that had not been treated properly.

I was able to keep myself going by staying busy, but my own recovery was not progressing very quickly. I didn't have to do that much at home because I now had a maid and four women in the house. I even had some free time to go for walks and to rest. At the beginning of February, 1946,

Stars and Chinese Coins

my neurologist arranged for me to go to a convalescent home in Switzerland for six weeks. It was a wonderful feeling to finally be somewhere without having to solve other people's problems. I was so happy that this doctor, about whom I had been so unhappy and uncertain, had arranged this trip for me. And Herman would be well taken care of by the women in the house.

I was going to leave in the middle of February, but first I definitely wanted to have Mr. Bräuel see a lung specialist. "Yes, of course," Dr. Smeding said. Mr. Bräuel was hard of hearing, so you had to shout when talking to him. And it was still impossible at the time to travel by bus with someone who spoke German. Later it turned out that I should have taken that risk.

While I was in Switzerland, my mother wrote me a letter weekly so I was always kept informed of the goings-on in the Netherlands. Of course, Herman also wrote regularly, but I could tell he was worrying too much and almost felt like a guest in his own home. The women were taking very good care of him, but apart from one corner in the study, the house had been taken over by the Russian Mennonites. My mother told me my youngest sister Nel had been admitted to the hospital in Leeuwarden with symptoms resembling rheumatism and my brother Pieter was in the hospital in Delft with typhus. This gave me quite a fright. I immediately thought of Mr. Bräuel and put two and two together. What if my brother and sister had contracted tuberculosis from Mr. Bräuel? I was so worried that I called Herman. And just as I thought, Dr. Smeding had not taken Mr. Bräuel to the lung specialist in Leeuwarden yet.

I was coming toward the end of my stay in Berne, and there was nothing I could do about Mr. Bräul's infectious illness anyway. But my worries did color those last few weeks. I had spent time in a totally different world at a level I greatly enjoyed. I had seen and learned all kinds of things and discovered that, despite my full life, there were still so many enriching experiences to have. And what would be waiting for me back home? Herman and I would be strangers. He would be swamped in work. The Russian Mennonites would be taking wonderful care of him. The closer the time came for me to go home, the more worried and tense I was.

I don't remember what I was feeling when I finally got there. Herman's clumsy embrace and his nervous way of doing things felt familiar. I was home again and would try to surround him with attention and care. I was

A clothing distribution center in Arnhem, where refugees came from morning until night, hoping to find something they could use.

glad to be there. Everyone sat at the table, ready to eat a festive Russian meal which had been prepared in my honor—borscht, pastry, wonderful delicacies, and lots of meat and fruit, compliments of Food for Relief from Canada and the States.

But all of my clothes had been divided up among the refugee women, who assumed I would die at the hospital! Although I didn't blame them, considering the survival mentality they had lived in for years, I have always been sad that my baptism dress which my grandmother made and embroidered for me had been cut into pieces.

One of the first things I asked Herman was whether Mr. Bräuel had been to Leeuwarden yet. He hadn't. I didn't want to lose my temper, but I was upset with the doctor who promised to take him there and disappointed that Herman had not done his best to make it happen. We were still eating when I announced that I wanted to take Mr. Bräuel to the Tuberculosis Clinic. He didn't look any worse than before, but the next morning I called the clinic and asked if we could come in.

One refugee remembers

On January 25, 1945, Gertrude Habegger and her family were given a few hours to leave their home in Prussia, a region of Germany during World War II. The Russian army was advancing west and this Mennonite family's farm would soon sit in a combat zone.

Gertrude, her mother, younger brother, and older sister left early that January morning and headed west, joining a slow-moving caravan of wagons fleeing the Russian army. "It was such a clear night and cold, and the snow was so high," Gertrude remembers. Her brother and sister took turns driving the horses, their hands wrapped in newspaper and gloves to fight off the cold.

As they left, they were ordered to resettle along a river in Germany. But with the Russian army only a day or two behind them, Else, Gertrude's sister, insisted that they continue west. With her strong sense of direction, Else drove through Germany until March 13, 1945, when they settled on a farm. Their wagon and horses were needed for fieldwork. Because of that, the family was given two rooms on the farm instead of being settled in a camp like many other refugees.

At a distribution center in a Mennonite church an hour away by train, Gertrude received a blue, flowered comforter made from feed bags. Though unfamiliar with comforters and quilts since she had used a featherbed in Prussia, Gertrude covered with the comforter on her bed at the farm. Later, she took it with her when she entered nurses training. And, finally, she opened the comforter and used the top and backing to make a dress. It was the only new dress she had and she wore it until it fell apart.

"It was such a comfortable dress," she says now.

Eventually, the family received a second comforter which Gertrude's mother wrapped around herself during the long boat ride from Germany to the United States after the War.

In 1953, Gertrude and her husband Eric emigrated to Ephrata, Pennsylvania, where her parents settled after the War. After her mother retired, she began working at Mennonite Central Committee's Material Resource Center (MRC), sewing hundreds of comforter tops that were sent to refugees around the world.

Working on comforters and quilts, plus focusing on the daily tasks of laundry and cooking, helped ease Gertrude and her mother's transition from Germany to the United States, Gertrude believes. Her father, who loved his work with horses in Prussia, found it more difficult to adapt to his new job in a concrete factory.

Gertrude continues to quilt and to coordinate the production of hundreds of comforters that are knotted twice a year by members of her congregation, Akron Mennonite Church.

We took the bus. Since Mr. Bräuel was hard of hearing, I told him we wouldn't talk. German was not the language people wanted to hear at the time. Everything went fine. Dr. Blanksma took a blood sample and X-rays. The results showed that Mr. Bräuel had a severe case of tuberculosis. In fact, he had only half a lung left. It was good to have my suspicions confirmed, but I was angry that nothing had been done to isolate him and prevent others from being infected. No one criticized us. Clearly we could not have known that our willingness to help might lead to this. But I felt we should have known better.

How responsible were we to protect the congregation and the village from someone with tuberculosis? We responded to whatever cries for help we heard and gave everyone who came to the door a place to stay. I suddenly felt very small and unhappy. Mr. Bräuel had to be isolated and no one could come into contact with him. I was relieved to have at least reached that decision.

Life went on. We got a call from the Mennonite Central Committee in Amsterdam who said that a large shipment of clothing was on its way for the villages around Irnsum. That was a job for me. We put everything on display in the shop across the street. Persons from each neighborhood and nearby village were invited to come and try on clothes, make a small donation to the church, and pick out what they wanted. There was an enor-

An MCC distribution center.

mous supply, though most of the women's shoes turned out to be too small. In America, where people didn't do much walking, the women had smaller, narrower feet. I was one of the lucky few who found something that fit. There were a lot of children's clothes, but they were too different from what we were used to. Our taste was still pretty much pre-War. The American look had not come into fashion yet.

The shipment of clothes arrived two days after I got back home. I couldn't go to Makkum, where my brother, Pieter, sister Nel, her boyfriend, and the two-year-old son of my sister Betsy were recuperating. The earlier diagnoses for each were wrong; when they heard about how they'd contracted tuberculosis, they were in the sunroom under piles of MCC quilts, brought to them by MCC distribution workers. I felt so guilty and ashamed that I hadn't been able to prevent them from being infected. What had we done? But no one criticized us. There was nothing to be done. Time had to do the healing—a great deal of patience and time. A year later, Pieter went to the sanatorium in Appelscha, and six months later Nel completed her recuperation in Switzerland. I was happy I could find a place for her to stay there with wonderful, hospitable people. She came back half a year later, completely recovered, but her engagement to marry had ended. I didn't know how to deal with that. I tried to make up for it by giving her extra attention.

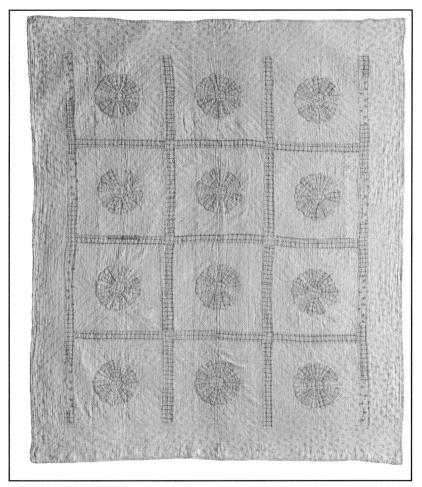

Dresden Plate

Hole in the Barn Door

Lynn
The quilts' journey

A handful of those quilts remain which served as bedding in An and Herman's home for the refugees fleeing Russia. They are pictured throughout this book as a kind of silent witness.

In the period when these quilts were made, women saved bits of clothing and pieced them together, leaving a kind of fingerprint—until the quilts wore out. Sometimes, as in this situation, these very personal articles were passed on to strangers in need. At least some of the quilts and comforters which An received from the MCC office were made much earlier than 1945. They clearly were not made for relief purposes but were family quilts, passed down from one generation to the next. But they were willingly offered when they were needed.

Where did these quilts come from? Here is what we've learned and what we know about the aid program of the Mennonite Central Committee (MCC) in Holland at the time.

As soon as the Occupation of Europe by Nazi forces began in 1939, Canadian Mennonites started collecting funds and clothing for English relief. England was the haven for streams of refugees from the Continent, so North Americans sent food, clothing, and blankets there for distribution to the incoming Europeans.

MCC started activities in England in 1940, and by 1943 they had opened a center which functioned as a clothing depot and hostel for children, as well as the administrative center and home for MCC personnel. In 1940, MCC sent its first collection of clothing to France, partially to clothe the Spanish refugees who crossed the border into France to escape the Spanish Civil War. By 1942, conditions had worsened to such an extent that relief goods could no longer be delivered to those places where they were most needed.

Loading relief clothing in Akron, Pennsylvania, in 1946 or 1947, to be taken to the clothing depot a few miles away in Ephrata.

* Irvin B. Horst, *A Ministry of Goodwill: A Short Account of Mennonite Relief 1939-1949* (Akron, PA: Mennonite Central Committee, 1950), 15.

Irvin Horst wrote in his short account, *A Ministry of Goodwill:* "When it became apparent that Mennonite and Brethren in Christ constituencies were ready to contribute large quantities of clothing and shoes, MCC set about to organize depots or centers for processing and storing the gifts. Such a center was first opened in a vacant Mennonite meetinghouse at Ephrata (Pennsylvania) in September, 1940 with Mrs. M. C. Lehman in charge. Until Mrs. Lehman went to Europe in 1945, she provided enthusiastic leadership for this aspect of Mennonite relief. She not only directed the cleaning, packing and storing of the goods but also visited the churches and encouraged the women to sew and donate all sorts of textile articles. As the work grew, a clothing processing center was opened at Kitchener, Ontario, in December, 1943, with Clara Snider in charge; a similar center was organized at Newton, Kansas, in September, 1944, with Mrs. Selma Linscheid as manager. Other centers were soon opened at Winnipeg, Manitoba, and at Reedley, California. But clothing and shoes were only one form of gifts-in-kind. Beginning with the successful trial shipment of canned food to Holland in 1945, MCC organized facilities to receive and ship an abundance of grain, flour, meat, fruit, vegetables and other food commodities which the churches contributed."*

The Mennonites of North American were gearing up to send significant amounts of help to occupied Europe, anticipating the War's end. Canadian Mennonites Peter and Elfrieda Dyck volunteered to go to England to do whatever would be helpful there, as well as to prepare for a massive relief program into the Continent, to be started as soon as conditions allowed.

When the southern parts of the Netherlands were liberated in 1944, some 500 Dutch children were evacuated to England to gain strength and to be put out of harm's way, should the Nazis be able to re-take their home area. The Dycks worked for three months at a camp in Hull, where they started to learn the Dutch language from the kids.

As MCC staff, Peter and Elfreida purchased transport equipment in England and sent two shipments of clothing from there to Holland. One 10-ton allotment shipped from MCC Canada was donated entirely to the Queen Wilhelmina Fund and went to Eindhoven in the south of Holland. This shipment included lots of quilts and comforters, which were apparently distributed among all those in need. A second shipment of clothing from the Kitchener MCC resource center got stuck in an English harbor for a while, finally reaching Amsterdam in December, 1945. By the end of that year, 1700 cases of home-processed foods, tomato paste, and assorted canned and dried foods had been consigned to Holland, as well as 22 carloads of wheat and flour, 965 bales of clothing, 47 cases of shoes, and 67 cases of soap.

These goods were sent in response to a letter from the Mennonite pastor, Rev. Gorter of Rotterdam, as well as other Dutch Mennonite communities who asked for help. Of course, emissaries and refugees from the area also carried word about what the Dutch people needed, so that MCC and other relief organizations could anticipate meeting their needs by gathering relief goods and holding them in depots.

Correspondence at the time from the MCC European relief director based in London, stated, "In regard to supplies we have here a large stock of clothing, some shoes, blankets and quilts that are ready to go. We would like to send the utility van loaded with supplies together with three workers to Holland as soon as permission can be secured from the Netherlands military authority" (MCC Archives).

Preparations continued in London, Canada, and the United States to have sufficient relief goods on standby and as close as physically possible to the Netherlands. London MCC worker Edna Hunsperger wrote to the MCC

Preparing quilts and comforters for shipping to Europe at the Ephrata, Pennsylvania, clothing center.

head office in Akron, Pennsylvania, on April 10, 1945, "Elma [Esau] and I have just returned from a lecture at Netherlands House on 'The Situation in Occupied Holland.' Our hearts were pained at the conditions we heard described by one who has recently been there in his native land. To know that there are four and a half million people so near us, now living, but starving . . . and many of whom will have succumbed before assistance can reach them. To us particularly, this is a very grave solemn fact, when we have resources of food and stocks of clothing to meet such needs."

Why did North American Mennonites focus on giving aid to Holland, instead of other European countries who were also suffering? Twenty-thousand Canadian Mennonites had been able to emigrate from Russia after the First World War, in large part because of financial help from the Dutch Mennonites. They wanted to repay a lifesaving favor, and, furthermore, they knew firsthand the horrors of war.

For the Mennonites of Lancaster County, Pennsylvania, an answer might be found in the history of their Swiss Anabaptist forebears who eventually settled in eastern Pennsylvania. John Landis Ruth writes about the history of support given centuries earlier by the Amsterdam and Rotterdam *Doopsgezinde* to the Swiss Anabaptists who were under siege. The Swiss state church was aligned with its government and saw any other form of worship as both religious competition and a threat to future tax rolls.

"A storm of protest began to arise in Amsterdam as the picture of Zurich's oppressions of its *Taeufer* (Anabaptists) became clear through readings of the 1639 reports. . . . What a contrast between the social liberties enjoyed by the Amsterdam *Doopsgezinde* and the marginal status of their free-church counterparts in Zurich! While the latter were languishing in prison, the former were gathering in a public meeting of some three thousand persons. At this time the Dutch, early leaders in worldwide colonization, were still the richest people in Christendom (Amsterdam serving as the hub of global commerce) . . . the Dutch *Doopsgezinde* convened in Amsterdam on February 24-25, 1710, to organize a new effort called Funds for Foreign Needs. This committee proved to be of historic and inestimable help to the ancestors of the Lancaster Mennonite conference. . . . One might see it as a foreshadowing of the twentieth-century American Mennonite Central Committee, with headquarters in prosperous Lancaster County, Pennsylvania. The Dutch organization was most timely; within a few weeks they heard that the promised mass expulsion of their spiritual relatives in Bernese prisons was about to be carried out."*

So an 18th-century emigration from Zurich and Berne left the heirs of the Swiss Mennonites with a debt of honor and gratitude to the Dutch two centuries later. Dutch generosity helped religious sisters and brothers reach a new world of religious freedom and opportunity. It is no wonder that the resource center that started in Ephrata, Pennsylvania, was able to gather and send so many tons of relief goods to Holland.

Soon after the May, 1945 Liberation, permission was given for MCC to come to Holland. Apart from the Liberation troops, MCC workers were the first non-Dutch to come to the Netherlands. Peter and Elfrieda Dyck sailed across the English Channel in June, 1945, just a month after the Netherlands were liberated. They loaded the van with all the relief goods they could manage to bring with them from London, including some quilts. A letter from an unattributed writer reports to MCC headquarters from London, "We had quite a send-off last week—Ellen Harder left Thursday for France with the usual fellow companion of at least one bicycle. The Dycks went off in the Holland van with Frieda driving. She was the only woman on the convoy and

* John Landis Ruth, *The Earth Is the Lord's: A Narrative History of the Lancaster Mennonite Conference* (Scottdale, PA: Herald Press, 2001), 68, 82, 158.

Centurion Martha Yoder
still stitching for relief

Months after celebrating her 101st birthday, Martha Yoder of Grantsville, Maryland, is still diligently working to help the needy. In her 99th year, she sewed 127 tops, and in her 100th year, 162 comforter tops. She donates many of these completed tops to local sewing circles. Eventually they make their way to refugees and victims of natural disasters around the world through Mennonite Central Committee (MCC).

Martha was born on August 14, 1903 near Meyersdale, Pennsylvania, and married Alvin H. Yoder on December 24, 1923. In 1928 they moved to Alvin's home farm in Grantsville, Maryland, where she still resides.

Martha was an active member of her church's sewing circle for many years. She particularly enjoyed sewing teddy bears, dresses, shirts, and trousers for Christmas bundles which were given where needed. She also made diapers and gowns for layette bundles. Sometimes she and other members of the sewing circle cut apart old coats and made them into smaller coats for needy children. She also remembers making mittens and caps.

Martha's husband, Alvin, was very supportive of her sewing. When the sewing circle met at a home other than her own, Alvin would transport her sewing machine with the cabinet to that home. Sometimes Martha and the sewing circle used printed feed bags for fabric. Alvin would go to a different mill than usual to buy feed if he thought the feed bags would be prettier there. Then he would often sort through the feed to find bags he particularly liked.

After Alvin suffered a debilitating stroke in 1980, Martha no longer attended sewing circle meetings. She cared for Alvin at home until his death in 1993. She continues to sew for others and praises God for her long and productive life.

had to drive a vehicle to rate that! The van was loaded—bicycles on the roof, and inside were all sorts of supplies imaginable—sewing machine, quilts, food, medical supplies, etc. etc."

Elfrieda describes what they saw when they awakened in the port of Ostende in Belgium the next morning, "At that point we were no longer in convoy and I was very relieved to hand the wheel over to Peter. . . . We made our way in the direction of Amsterdam. Many bridges were out so we couldn't cross. Then we had to go over pontoon bridges and that's a wobbly experience. There were a lot of potholes in the roads from the bombing and military travel with tanks. . . . It was not normal travel by any means. No gas stations and a lot of ruins, whole villages destroyed. We were driving through a battlefield after the guns had been silenced. It was shocking and depressing. We spent Saturday night on the road somewhere. Sunday afternoon we arrived in Amsterdam and reported to the Mennonite Church, 452 Singel."

The custodian gave them a tour of the historic Mennonite church where the ADS (*Algemeene Doopsgezinde Societeit*), the Dutch Mennonite Confer-

Utilizing the flour sacks required help from all the refugees harbored in an Amsterdam-area home. The boys shake the sacks before they're washed.

ence, has its offices and where later MCC had its office on the second floor. Built in 1608, it had been a hidden church. "One entered the church through an ordinary house that faced the street. After the persecution in the 16th century, Mennonites were tolerated but were not to be visible," writes Peter Dyck.

Monkey Wrench

The official organization of the Dutch Mennonites (the ADS) appointed a committee of three to counsel and advise the MCC workers: Dr. H. Craandijk, secretary of the Dutch Mennonite Society, G. H. Rahusen, and Rev. T. O. Hylkema, An and Herman's friend.

Soon the Dycks were settled into a house on Murillostraat and were able to welcome new MCC workers and distribute the first major shipment of clothing after it arrived at the port of Rotterdam. The major relief distribution program had to wait—tons and tons of relief goods were delayed for two months due to labor strikes in the American ports.

Peter Dyck wrote about the distribution of relief goods in his "Report on MCC Relief Activities in Holland from July 20, 1945-June 20, 1946, " . . . MCC had an agreement with HARK, which is charged with the responsibility of distributing all relief clothing and shoes coming to the Netherlands. This agreement calls for a distribution to Mennonites and to non-Mennonites on a fifty-fifty basis. (Please note that in actual practice it has worked out to a ratio of 40:60 in favor of non-Mennonites.) We would go from town to town, staying approximately a week in each town, distributing in a concentrated manner. The Mennonites would be contacted through the local Mennonite church; the non-Mennonites through the regional HARK office or through Volksherstel which is akin to HARK. (Within this period, a total of 44,200 people had been served; the average number of people served with one bale of clothing was 44.)"

"One day, while standing at the docks watching another ship being unloaded, the director of the Dutch Red Cross turned to me and said, 'I didn't know that almost half the people of the United States and Canada are Mennonites,'" recounts Peter Dyck in *Up from the Rubble*. "I laughed and asked, 'What made you say that?' He replied, 'Because almost half of all the relief supplies coming to Holland these days are from the Mennonite Central Committee.'"*

So where did the quilts come from which An was sent? And from where were they shipped? We can only guess. Elfrieda and Peter brought some quilts with them from England. Because there was so little space in the van, we might surmise that these quilts were especially needed, and may have come out of the first shipments to England from Canada.

On the other hand, shipments from the U.S. had been distributed widely before An asked for blankets in 1946. (Twenty tons were handed out in

* Peter and Elfrieda Dyck, *Up from the Rubble* (Scottdale, PA: Herald Press, 1991), 60.

November and December, 1945, alone.) At the time, Peter Dyck reported that there were blankets in abundance. Short of finding a person who recognizes the quilts from these pictures, the exact origin of these 19 quilts will never be known.

Sometimes, items packed into bales in North America were recognized when unpacked in Amsterdam. In a letter addressed to "Dear Friends of the Clothing Centers in the U.S.A." and dated January 19, 1945, one woman wrote from Amsterdam, "Exactly two years to the very day after I packed my first bale at Ephrata, I opened one which I, myself, had packed (there)— in Amsterdam, Holland! That was a real thrill! Since then, I've opened many of my own bales and have recognized clothing from Ephrata, Newton, and Kitchener. When is the big yellow dress coming through? I'm looking forward to that day. The Dutch are always complaining that our American clothing is too small, and for once, we'd like to have something on hand too big for anyone! And we often wondered how the coats, comforters, suits and other clothing would look after it had been pressed so long in the bales. It

Women from the Maple Glen Mennonite Church near Grantsville, Maryland, knotting a comforter, mid- to late 1940s.

Quilts and comforters nearly ready for shipping to Europe in the Ephrata, Pennsylvania, clothing center.

looks just wonderful. The bedding soon loses all indications of having been pressed. And the woolens, too, look remarkably smooth. The paper keeps the bales nice and clean. In fact, the bales look very much as they do when they are at the home clothing centers. There's no evidence whatever of that burlap-bag-freight-dust-and-grime we sometimes experienced at the center at home."

Once the most primary needs had been alleviated, Peter Dyck tried to assess how best to distribute the tons of relief goods still on hand. Some 90,000 Dutch political prisoners had been rounded up after the War to be charged with collaborating with the Nazi enemy. They were separated from their children and kept in custody until their cases could be examined. Twenty thousand of these innocent but now stigmatized children had to wait in special camps for their parents' release from custody. The children need-ed clothes and food, and the Dutch government was "quite favorable to the help of outside groups." Large distributions were made to these children's camps. It is likely that many of them slept under Mennonite-made quilts and comforters.

I have been able to find only one other individual who received a quilt or blanket during this time, and then kept it:

Mrs. J. Vis-Hartog of Wisserkerke writes: "In Amsterdam, I was given an MCC quilt just after the War. Actually, my parents got it via the Singel

Church in Amsterdam, but my mother thought that I should have it. The top had a purple and black design and it was lined with wool. The whole quilt was stitched through, and I slept under it for a very long time. It was a very simple design but I was always very pleased with it—especially so soon after the War's end and as a 14-year-old girl.

"The letters 'MCC' meant a lot to me. There was also an MCC center in Amsterdam on the Koningslaan, where I often came and sang. I told any American guests there about my 'rag blanket' with pride; the word 'quilt' was not then so well known."

Most of the quilts were apparently sent to large institutions and centers where hundreds of persons slept and where those quilts stayed. The first 33 Russian émigrés slept under quilts at Fredeshiem. Ans Knipscheer-Smid, a Dutch woman, wrote a letter about her memories of sleeping under quilts while attending events at the Mennonite retreat center at Elspeet: "For many years, relief quilts decorated the beds and warmed the sleepers there."

"Just to look out on the street, one does not think the clothing situation is so bad. The people seem quite well-dressed, but on closer inspection one notices how much their hose are mended, that their shoes are badly worn and that the clothing is often made over—yes, even dresses out of tablecloths and bedspreads. However, they are very neat so that one must look closely to see the mends. One of Craandijk's daughters said it had been three years since she had had a pair of shoes. She said that it was their underwear which showed the most wear and the clothing of her little sister, who had grown out of all her clothing. Many children wear clogs and wooden soled sandals which their parents have made. Some have the toe cut out of their leather shoes because they have become too small. Everywhere one sees shops for repairing or making over clothing."

Signed, Elma Esau
September 10, 1945, Holland

Rectangle

Lynn

Lynn
Surprise at the border

The MCC crew had come to the Netherlands to help the Dutch people with food and fiber. No one expected the arrival of hundreds of Russian Mennonite refugees in late 1945, who needed to be cared for as well.

The Dycks arrived in Amsterdam in June, 1945, ahead of relief supplies and MCC workers. While staying at the home of Dr. Craandijk, one of the advisors to MCC, they used the time to find a house to serve as a center and to furnish it. This was a problem, as the stores were empty. There were no furnishings to buy. But the city of Amsterdam made furniture available that had been confiscated from NSB collaborators. Elfrieda Dyck reports, "Amsterdam had large warehouses full of NSB furniture and household equipment. I had to list what we needed and then was directed to a warehouse to pick it up." About a year later, a house was made available on Koningslaan when the Canadian forces pulled out. This house, too, had been requisitioned from NSBers. How ironic it was to use furniture sat on by the enemy, who had perhaps taken those very goods from Jewish homes.

In August, Rev. Hylkema's sister sent him a newspaper clipping from Maastricht, a city on the German border. Thirty-three people had come to the border between Germany and Holland, telling a story of having left Holland 400 years ago, all poor, but sure that they would return someday. Now they were here, claiming to have come home, begging to be allowed to stay. They spoke a kind of broken Dutch, and yet it wasn't Dutch. The Queen was told their story and she gave them permission to enter the country. Then the press became interested and picked up the story, and so Hylkema's sister sent the article to him in Amsterdam.

As Hylkema read the newspaper clipping, he became more and more excited. Peter Dyck recalls, "He came right over to the MCC center to Elfrieda and me. 'Here, look at this, look, look! Are these not Mennonites from the Ukraine, are these not our people?' We read it and said, it sure sounds that way. We immediately made a plan to go at once and personally investigate on the spot in Maastricht. The article was inconclusive—a decision had not been made yet that they would be allowed to stay in Holland. Immediately we took to the road.

"When we got to the large camp with many refugees of various descriptions, the camp leader told us where the group we sought usually huddled together. We saw them before they saw us. And just the way the women had their kerchiefs around their heads, the way they sat and talked to each other, the way the men stood there, their features . . . and then as we came closer and listened to their language, why, before I was introduced, I

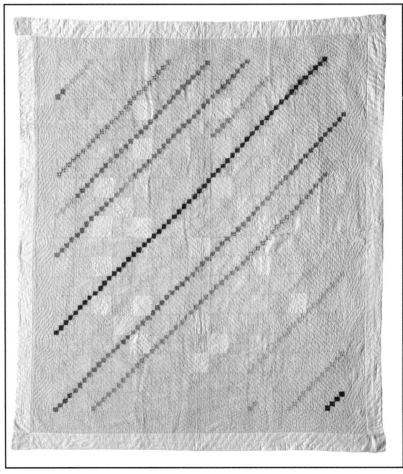

Double Four-Patch with Diagonal Squares

already thought, ninety-nine percent certain, these are our people. These are *Plautdietsch* people like peas out of the same pod with us.

"So we walked up and Dominee Hylkema introduced himself. As far as they were concerned, he was just another Dutchman. But the moment I spoke *Plautdietsch* to them and told them my name, and that I was also born in Russia, was now a Canadian, the contact was established and everything was clear, to us and to them. So we went to the camp leader and simply told him our discovery: they are Dutch *Doopsgezinde* (Anabaptists) who fled from Holland under persecution in the 16th century and who have fled again under persecution from Russia back to Holland. We requested that they do nothing drastic with these people until they heard again from us. Then Hylkema and I went to The Hague to talk to people in the Dutch government.

"Once we had established trust, the Russian émigrés told how they had left the Ukraine, fleeing ahead of the retreating German army. At first they had been happy when the Germans arrived—they saw them as liberators after the hard years under Russian anarchists and later Communists. But disillusionment set in when they observed the Germans' cruel treatment of Jews and their arrogance towards the Russian people.

"So after the battle of Stalingrad when the German army retreated westward, they fled to get out of Russia. They didn't want to go to Germany—they had never been in Germany, but many had relatives in Canada, where 20,000 of their family members had immigrated after WWI. All of this spilled out at the first meeting with the first thirty-three refugees.

"They also said that thousands more like themselves were coming westward, hoping to go to Canada. (It was later established that some 35,000 Russian Mennonites survived the journey out of Russia, out of the 125,000 who initially fled. But at least 23,000 of these were forcibly returned to Russia. Thousands more died on the way. Only a couple of thousand survived the trek and settled in Paraguay, Canada and Germany.)"

The first 33 who arrived in Maastricht on the German-Dutch border were moved to Fredeshiem, a Mennonite retreat center, by MCC staff in army surplus trucks which MCC had bought. The MCCers helped them settle in, found clothes for them, as well as work on nearby farms, and got the younger children enrolled in school.

Officieele mededeelingen over vertrek en aankomst.
Official notes of departure and arrival.
Offizielle Abreise- und Ankunftmitteilungen.

Officieele mededeelingen over vertrek en aankomst.
Official notes of departure and arrival.
Offizielle Abreise- und Ankunftmitteilungen.

DRUK DE BUSSY, AMSTERDAM

NEDERLANDSCHE

MENNO-PAS

Verklaring omtrent
**Nederlandsche afkomst en
toelating in Nederland**

Declaration of
**Dutch origin and
permit to enter Holland**

Angabe
Holländische Herkunft und
Aufnahmeerlaubnis in Holland

Bewaar dezen pas zorgvuldig.
Guard this pass well.
Diesen Pasz persönlich behalten, nicht abgeben!

A

№ ....

Verklaring omtrent
Declaration of

Nederlandsche afkomst
Dutch origin

en *and*

toelating in Nederland
permit to enter Holland

betreffende: *concerning:*

naam }
name } ....

geboren *born* ....

laatstelijk wonende: *last recidence:*

Handteekening
Signature of bearer

B

De A.D.S., Algem. Doopsgez. Societeit in Nederland
Het M.C.C., Mennonite Central Committee U.S.A.
& Canada

verklaren dat de in A genoemde persoon
declare that the person named in section A

....

is: Doopsgezinde van Nederlandsche afkomst
is: Mennonite of Dutch origin

en dat zij voor hem (haar) zullen zorg dragen in
Nederland en bij de emigratie naar Canada,
*and that they will care for him (her) in Holland
and for the emigration to Canada,*

Overeenkomstig beschikking van den Commandant
According to the order of the Commander

van de Grensbewaking in Nederland v. 22 Dec. 1945
of the Frontier Guard in Holland of 22 Dec. 1945

heeft deze persoon: *this person has:*

toestemming in Nederland binnen te komen.
permission to enter Holland.

Voor de A.D.S. en het M.C.C.

Datum:

C

VOOR DE GRENSAUTORITEITEN IN NEDERLAND

De Beschikking van den Commandant der Grensbewaking te dezer zake luidt aldus:

„DIENST DER GRENSBEWAKING

Ondergeteekende, Commandant der Grensbewaking
geeft bij dezen toestemming om in Nederland toe te
laten transporten Russische doopsgezinden van Hol-
landsche afkomst, welke binnenkomen te Maastricht,
Eindhoven of Enschede, die als gewone repatrieerenden
moeten worden beschouwd.

Deze personen moeten in het bezit zijn van een verklaring afgegeven door Ds. T. O. Hylkema of een
anderen vertegenwoordiger namens de A.D.S. in Nederland en de M.C.C. (Mennonite Relief U.S.A. & Canada)
welke de verzorging van deze menschen in Nederland
en de emigratie naar Canada op zich genomen hebben.

DEN HAAG, 22 December 1945

De Kolonel der Kon. Marechaussee
Commandant der Grensbewaking
w.g. H. G. VAN EVERDINGEN"

Commandant Grensbewaking
C. O. Frontier Guard

Grensautoriteiten of Repatrieeringsdienst in Nederland
worden verzocht bij aankomst van deze persoon in een
repatrieeringskamp daarvan bericht te zenden aan de
A.D.S.-M.C.C., Singel 457, Amsterdam-C.

The Menno Pass, required for the Russian Mennonites to enter the Netherlands.

SURPRISE
AT THE BORDER

More refugees kept coming, and soon Fredeshiem was so full that the ADS began placing them in private homes throughout Friesland's villages and farming communities. People offered to open their homes, and so the ADS took a survey to discover who would be willing to receive Mennonite refugees. Elfrieda recalls, "One might think that putting them into private homes should be no problem because there were thousands of Dutch Mennonites, but we must remember they had just barely survived the war. They had nothing. Everything was rationed. They were not yet back on their own feet, and for them to take in these people was a very, very difficult undertaking. It required a lot of altruism. But many did. That's a story that has never been told."

After Fredeshiem was full and the available homes had been filled, more refugees kept coming. The Dutch committee and MCC rented a big country house called Roverestein and installed 200 people there. The first 33 were also moved there, so that the Dutch Mennonites could once again use their retreat center, Fredeshiem. After about 450 Russian Mennonites had entered the country on Menno Passes, the border was suddenly closed, never to open again to them. The closure was the consequence of pressure brought to bear on the Dutch government by Russians, who read the newspaper coverage about this unusual group of people. The Russian government still controlled the movement of some 12,000 Dutch citizens, mostly forced laborers, and threatened to forbid their return home unless the Dutch turned over the Russian "traitors." Dutch government officials had to allow them to interview the Mennonites, but only under the condition that they would be asked if they wanted to return. If they did not want to return, they would not have to go back. None wanted to return, but the Dutch had to agree either to terminate the Menno Pass means to sanctuary or to betray their own citizens who were trying to get home from Russia.

Herman and An in the garden of their retirement home.

An—1947
The Ukrainian Mennonites leave Irnsum

*I*t was an eventful year in Irnsum. The Ukrainian Mennonites would be leaving for Paraguay on a big ship, but the date still had not been set and they were getting nervous. They were finally taken to Rotterdam in a couple of trucks in late January, 1947. Altogether there were more than a hundred of them staying in various towns in Friesland. The ship, the Volendam, was moored in Rotterdam and was going to go past Bremen, Germany, to pick up another group there. Their departure was delayed because it was difficult to get free transit passes for the refugees in Berlin since the city was divided into four occupied zones (American, British, French, and Russian). With a great deal of zeal, Peter and Elfrieda Dyck of MCC prayed that the ship could cross the ocean. In the end, they all did manage to leave.

Even when the ship was already at sea, it was uncertain whether Mr. Bräuel would be able to get past the health inspectors once they arrived in Paraguay. But he was admitted to the country and lived for another two years with only one-third of a lung. The others on the ship had probably been in contact with tuberculosis and were resistant. I never heard anyone mention it again. The voyage was long and there were horrible storms on the way, but these people's firm belief in God accompanied them to their new homeland.

I came home after the operation on my back just before our guests were about to leave, so it wasn't a good idea for me to go to Rotterdam to see them off, but I went anyway. We all went on board the ship the first night we got there and slept in hammocks in the hull. It was a new experience and I didn't get much sleep. I remember standing on the pier the next morning and waving to them, tiny and insignificant next to the huge ship that slowly moved away from the land, making its way to a distant country and an uncertain future. The only thing these fugitives knew for sure was that they would not be persecuted in Paraguay, and they would be able to practice their religion in freedom with members of their church who had emigrated before them.

It was a somber day in Rotterdam, foggy, with wet winds blowing. We took the train home.

I felt like I was coming into a totally unfamiliar house. I had to find a place for myself all over again. The house was cold and empty. We crawled into bed together. It was already late by the time we got on the train to come home. I had cried all my tears at the pier and on the way home, as I thought about the uncertain future of our Mennonite brothers and sisters who had been through so much. We fell asleep without a word. We promised each other that starting tomorrow, we would be together in a different way, more focused on each other no matter how much my back ached. We wanted to build a life together, and we would start by turning the parish back into our own home.

Herman got up bright and early. When I came downstairs, the heater was on in his study. We had a nice quiet breakfast together and I urged that we would take the whole day just for ourselves. With our maid Sietske, we started to restore the house to what it had been like before. We polished, vacuumed, dusted, and put everything back exactly where we wanted it. We returned the stove to the rear room. Herman turned it on right away to clear the clammy, humid air and to make the spacious room a pleasurable place to spend time. Even though the furniture was not exactly my taste, we rearranged it around the stove. Exhausted but with satisfaction, we had a cup of tea together at the end of the afternoon and then ate our meal. I don't remember what we had, but it was probably Food for Relief in every sense.

Years later we heard that Rev. Postma and his brother-in-law Luijtens, who had collaborated with the Germans, were on the Volendam with their families. I don't know whether Postma took the job of chaplain on board. The Mennonite Central Committee had asked Herman to serve on the ship as chaplain and to go on from Rio to Australia accompanying the people who wanted to return to the Netherlands from the Netherlands East Indies, which was soon to become Indonesia. Herman did not feel he could abandon his communities back home, but how much experience and spiritual wisdom he would have gained and brought to his work had we done that. It would have been a wonderful opportunity to add to our limited experience and expand our horizons. Yet I was determined that we would make a new start together.

After the Ukrainians were gone, Herman and I sat looking at each other on the couch and asked, "What now?" We hardly knew each other as individuals, the years had been so turbulent.

Years of pastoral work and child-rearing soon followed, and I never talked again about the traumatic experiences in what should have been my youth.

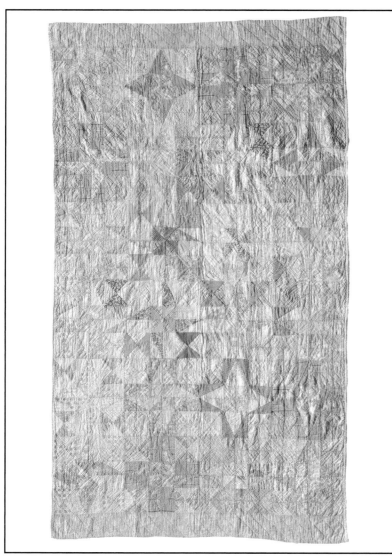

Stars and Triangles

Lynn and An

An—1980
Lynn meets the quilts; I meet Lynn

*I*n 1980 our daughter Anke threw a party at our house in Borg for a group of her student friends. A Palestinian classmate of hers enjoyed the party and asked whether he and some relatives and friends could get together there sometime. Of course it would be possible for them to spend a weekend at Borg. I did not have to think twice about it. He and his friends were far from home, living and studying all over Europe. I asked how many people he was thinking of inviting. He said about 15. The house could accommodate them; in fact, I had put our chest of old, worn quilts there, and said they could use them if they needed them. Anke's friend Samir was in touch with me right after their weekend at the house to say that they had had a great party!

That very evening I got a phone call from a young woman who sounded quite emotional. In a mixture of poor Dutch and English, she said she had been to Borg for a weekend with her Palestinian family. She told me she had slept under a quilt that reminded her of her parents' home and of her great-grandmother. These were the quilts we had used for the Ukrainian Mennonites, five of whom spent a year at our house in Irnsum. The woman on the phone asked if she could buy the quilt. That was out of the question, I said. The quilts had been given to me as a gift, and so I couldn't sell them. But I could give her one if it meant so much to her. She would have to come and show me which one she was interested in.

I sensed that there was a story behind her call. But she didn't come, and every year when I opened the chest to air out the quilts, I felt a pang of guilt. The young woman had been so upset. But I didn't know who she was or where she lived. I didn't know how to reach her.

Nine years and nine months later the phone rang, and I heard a very cheerful voice asking if I remembered her. "I didn't come and I didn't call, but I haven't forgotten anything. It was nine years and nine months ago

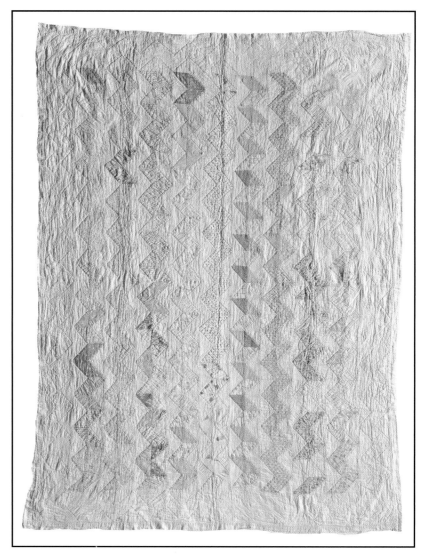

Zigzag

that I first spoke to you." I immediately made the connection and the ice was broken. Lynn asked if she could borrow all my quilts for an exhibition at their family bookshop.

I was surprised and wondered how to go about this, but I thought it would certainly be feasible. Lynn said she could pick the quilts up on a Sunday afternoon in the beginning of November.

Lynn speaking at an exhibit of the quilts.

It turned out to be an emotional afternoon with a lot of stories. Lynn wanted to exhibit the quilts in the store over Thanksgiving and invited us to come celebrate the holiday with her and her family. Anke joined Herman and me, hoping to meet her friend Samir there, the young man who had been the link to Lynn.

Anke, Herman, and I drove from Friesland to Amsterdam. While Herman was parking the car, Anke and I walked up the Kalverstraat, looking for the numbers on the buildings that are sometimes hard to see

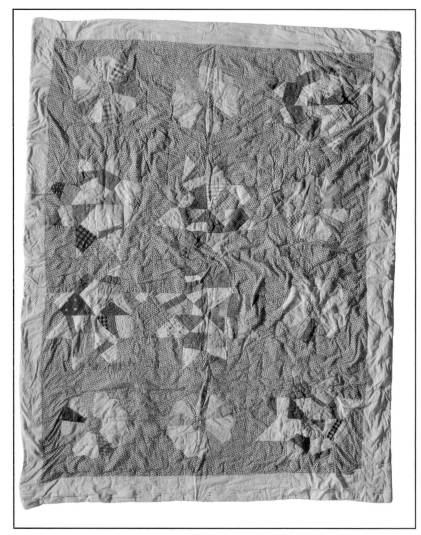

Crazy Stars and Dresden Plates

because of all the advertising. Wondering how far we had to go, we saw a group of people standing in front of a window. We were about to walk on when my eye caught something familiar. We had obviously found the right address.

We entered what turned out to be a huge bookshop and took the elevator to the fourth floor, a large space where the quilts were exhibited very professionally. My heart opened up. Here the quilts were on display to their best advantage, showing their true worn beauty. I was impressed. We finished the day with a Thanksgiving dinner with Lynn and her husband and children.

Lynn was a very busy businesswoman, so after that we kept in touch by telephone. The quilts were always what kept us connected. We visited her and her family in Landsmeer, usually when Herman was preaching at the Mennonite church there. And over time, she learned the story of how I got the quilts and why they meant so much to me.

Lynn did not know in 1980, when she spent the weekend in Borg, that she was staying at the home of a Mennonite minister and his family. Nor did she know that the Dutch word *Doopsgezind* is used for "Mennonites" in the Netherlands. (In the Frisian language we say *Mennist*.) During all her years in Amsterdam, she had never made that link. If she had come to Friesland as soon as she arrived in the Netherlands, she wouldn't have had to live for years without her faith community. Lynn returned the quilts to us after the exhibition, and we stored them on the landing again in Borg.

An speaking at an exhibit of the quilts.

Lynn and Avo

Lynn—June 1980
Discovering Mennonites in Holland

I wasn't looking for Mennonites. Busy with two jobs and two kids without grandparents from either Avo's side or mine, we relied on help from two women. Nel helped in our home with cleaning and babysitting. Agnes offered day care in her home for young children up to the age of kindergarten. They had both met my parents on one of their trips over from Minnesota, and one day Agnes asked me if my background was by any chance *"Doopsgezind?"* After we figured out together that the name probably meant "Anabaptist," rather than "Baptist," and that it might indicate followers of Menno Simons, I made the connection. "Well," she said, "the new Mennonite minister brings her boys to me for day care. Would you like me to introduce you?" I would and she did.

One evening Ruth Hoogewoud, the Mennonite pastor, rode up on her bicycle. First over coffee, then over wine, we traded background stories and she invited me to come to the church services. I didn't get there until around Christmas time, and what a different experience that was from my childhood church experiences. For one thing, the children stayed in the service except during the sermon, and they were asked to respond to questions from the pulpit and read a picture book quietly in their seats.

The music had an older, irregular-sounding cadence, although the texts were similar. There was a choir made up of only women, and it creaked like the wooden stairs one climbed to the balcony. The building was more than 100 years old and sagged. One window frame had come loose from the shifting walls, leaving a triangular gap which some able carpenter filled by reframing the window with a trapezoidal pane. The whole place had a musty, mossy smell and yet the people were so warm. Probably only about 35 adults were there, but I was greeted, asked my name, and given coffee afterwards.

I didn't go back for a long while. Then one spring, I got to longing for conversations about more than sail surf boards and vacation destinations. I

Coffee-time at a Dutch Mennonite church.

snuck into the balcony of a Dutch Protestant church to hear the service. I found the sermons there to be like collegiate lectures, very well constructed logically and filled with explication of key words in the chosen text. But no one ever said hello. I felt like a spectator, not a participant. One summer Sunday morning, I had an intense longing to go to church, so I went back, but when I got there, the building was empty. I remembered that they had combined services with the Dutch Reformed congregation for the summer period. I went to their church building and could hear voices singing inside, but the door was locked. That seemed strange.

So I drove a mile down the road to the *Doopsgezinde* congregation, walked in late, was greeted anyway, and the service went on around me. The city had condemned the building. Faced with renovation or replacement, the small congregation had decided to tear down the old building and build a new one. This was a courageous act, since the number of *Doopsgezinde* was shrinking all over the Netherlands after World War II. Churches were being sold to local governments to become civic centers, not built anew. So I sat there, feeling quite excited about being able to be of some use, and yet afraid

DISCOVERING
MENNONITES
IN HOLLAND
160

that I was not evangelical enough or good enough or Dutch enough to be accepted.

As soon as the service was over, a spry little old lady with red-brown curls, called out, "Hey, Lynn! How are you?" We had coffee amidst a lot of people doing all kinds of planning and visiting. It was a cozy kind of busyness. No one pushed me in any way (which would have sent me running), but it was clear I could participate if I wished.

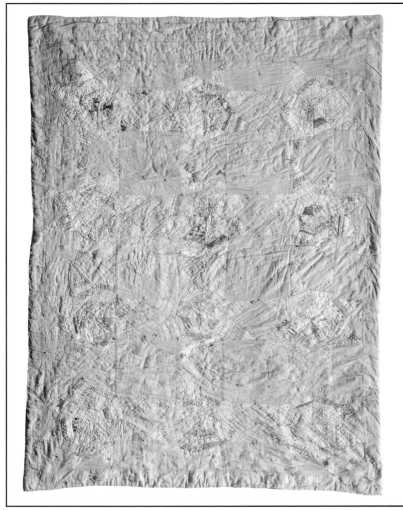

String Stars

I started to come, at first alone, then later with the children. I wanted them to have a knowledge of the Bible stories and also contact with some Dutch elders, since their own were unavailable. For Avo, grown up in the Eastern Orthodox tradition, the Mennonite church building and services were too bare. So the kids and I went to the services, held every other week, and to the farewell party for the old building.

Garden furniture and sun parasols replaced the normal chairs in the sanctuary. Summer food was set out and we sang funny songs to the accompaniment of an accordion player and his cohorts wearing silly hats. The party started with a prayer and ended with a shared clean-up effort.

I took instruction class in a large Mennonite church in Minnesota at age 15 with about 30 other adolescents. We were too young to realize, I think, what we were committing ourselves to. The teaching was classical in style—we had workbooks where we were to answer questions based on a short text about Mennonite history or theology. Three main items stuck with me that distinguish Mennonite/Anabaptist theology from many other Christian groups:

- Adult baptism. Rather than baptizing infants in order to "save" their souls, baptism follows a personal confession of faith when an applicant is old enough to understand at least a degree of what s/he is committing to.
- Refusal to bear arms or to swear an oath. The teaching of Jesus to "give to Caesar that which is Caesar's" stops short of killing others on Caesar's behalf.
- The Minister is no more holy than other members of the faith community. No fancy vestments are worn by the minister which might indicate God's extra favor. All members are equal in standing with God and can talk directly to him always, whether man or woman.

Here was a church which read the Bible as a guide for living, and then set about in plain and silent ways to discuss and discover the way to go. There were no fewer than seven Mennonite congregations in that small Minnesota town of 2,000 people, most of them emigrants from centuries-old settlements in the Ukraine. The villagers still spoke 16th-century *Plautdietsch* (commonly known as Low German) among themselves. The first service each Sunday was in High German; the second in Low German. English serv-

A Dutch Mennonite church building in Friesland.

ices began only in about 1960. Although I wasn't part of the church's social setting because we lived in an "English" village about an hour's drive away, I liked the group's theology.

I discovered that the Mennonites in the Netherlands, who did not flee as my foreparents did, have a slightly different theological emphasis and lifestyle. My people were immigrants, who, like most immigrants, hung onto the old language and old patterns in a threatening outside world. The Dutch Mennonites who didn't emigrate through the period of persecution and martyrdom were fully assimilated Dutch citizens and helped to develop the Dutch economy as food-processors, textile-weavers, shipbuilders, tradesmen, and financiers. They were cultural insiders, even leaders by the 18th century.

In Europe, members of little-known religious minorities were tolerated only if they behaved discreetly. World War II highlighted the vulnerability of minority religious groups. Perhaps this helps explain the emphasis on individual, private beliefs among Dutch Mennonites, which contrasts so clearly with the group-held and openly communicated beliefs of their North American counterparts.

Dutch Mennonites express their beliefs in this way:
"Baptize those who are adult;
Don't use too may words;
Freedom of Christian belief;
Deeds are above words."

An and Lynn

An—1992
What to do with the quilts?

In 1992, we had a beautiful summer, which made bearable the fact that I had to spend three months in a bed on our terrace because of the pinched nerve in my back. The pain was excruciating and I could scarcely move, yet I had an opportunity to reflect on things. We were living in Borg, a great house with no neighbors close by, and so a bit lonely. I began to wonder if we should leave this house. Herman dismissed the idea, but I kept thinking about the possibility that something could go wrong. I didn't want to become a burden to our neighbors, and the idea grew within me of moving to a smaller house in the small town of Drachten. Herman slowly accepted this idea.

In 1994 we would celebrate our fiftieth anniversary, and I wondered if that might be a good time to move. I thought about the chest of quilts, of course. A quilt guild had approached me a few times to say they would like to put the quilts on display at their museum in Tilburg. They also wanted to publish an article about them in their magazine.

The date of our move was approaching and I knew I had to decide on a place for the quilts. I remembered the museum in Tilburg, but for some reason that idea did not appeal to me. I was too emotional about the quilts.

One Sunday when Herman was preaching in Landsmeer, we had lunch with Lynn and Avo. Avo told us that he wanted to give Lynn a memorable gift that year for some reason or another. "Can you help me?" he asked.

I remembered our visit to the

Avo

The Mennonite Church in Irnsum.

Mennonite meetingplace in Irnsum, which had had its entrance renovated. The church had been nearly restored otherwise except for some repairs which had to be postponed because of lack of funds. The rear section of the building had been one of the first secret churches. The windows in that part of the structure needed to be replaced. I thought of Lynn who visited us periodically, but whom I had always refused to answer when she mentioned the quilts. I knew I had to make a decision. If she would pay for the windows . . . she would have her heart's desire and so would we.

The Mennonites in Irnsum definitely needed financial assistance to replace the windows in their church. And Irnsum was our first parish and our first love. I asked Avo if he would pay for the windows. Herman was planning a commemorative service because Irnsum was his first parish and he had begun there as a minister 50 years earlier. We had also received the quilts while we lived in the Irnsum church's parsonage. At the service, I could give Lynn the quilts. Then we would have come full circle. I drew a breath of relief.

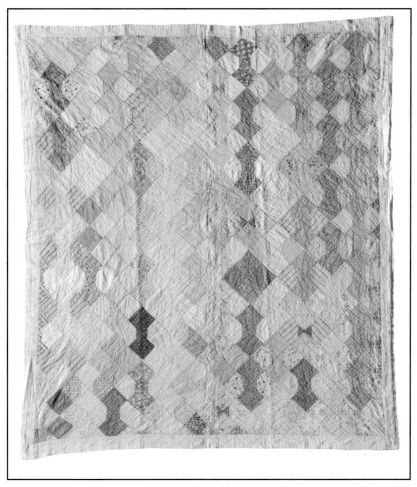

Bowties

I asked Herman what he thought of the idea. He was glad I had decided what to do with the quilts. And so that is how the transfer of the quilts took place. Our children knew how attached I was to the quilts, and the three of them were able to attend the special event we planned.

After briefly explaining to the parish what happened in 1946, I gave Lynn the chest of quilts. The church council received the envelope with a check from Avo for new windows. It was a very emotional moment for Lynn and for me. We are both so happy that this solution was given to us—and that is how we each perceive our relationship and the quilts—as gifts.

On that September day in 1994, when we were all having coffee after the service, a man named Folkert approached me and said that this was also the fiftieth anniversary of his release from prison. He had been the first Underground detainee to be released from prison and sent home to Irnsum soon after we arrived there. Surprised, I had forgotten that the Resistance was so active in 1944—so it was my anniversary, too!

An and Herman with their children (left to right), Anke, Jan, and Ton Keuning, at the celebration of Herman's 50 years as a minister.

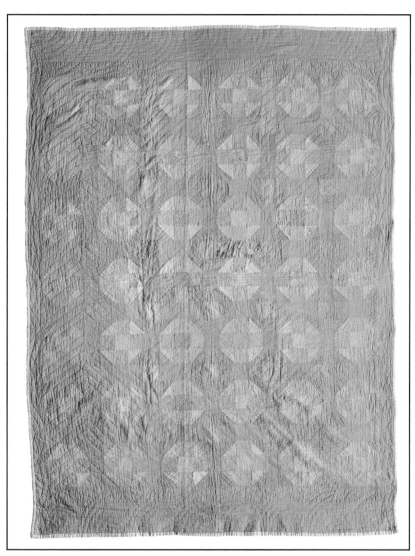

Shoo-Fly

Left to right: Nadine holding Amir, Avo, Lynn, and Paul

Lynn—September 1994
Stewarding the quilts

*O*ur drive to Friesland on the morning of Herman's anniversary celebration—and the event when An would hand the quilts to me for safekeeping—was emotionally exhausting. Avo was going through a delayed grieving process, having just returned from his first trip to visit his parents' graves in Syria. He wasn't sure whether he belonged in the Middle East or in Holland. I worried about him and couldn't soften his sorrow. His sadness made me sad and I was also concerned about the future of our family. We talked in the car, caught up in emotion, and missed a turn to the village. Suddenly it looked like we would arrive late.

Always in awe of the circumstances which had brought me into An's life, and nervously grateful for the trust she was placing in me to preserve the quilts and to tell their stories, I hated arriving late. I was afraid we would seem disrespectful. It wasn't lack of respect on our part, only entanglement. Life in our household was never simple. It seemed harder to do the right thing for our children because of our very different cultural backgrounds and assumptions as the kids became teenagers. A simple thing like getting up on time, and getting to an unknown village to help mark the passing of a chapter in the lives of people now dear to us, triggered powerful emotions. Lost, both of us crying, we suddenly saw a complete double rainbow to the left of the road. The sky is big in Friesland, as wide and overwhelming as the sky above my hometown. Seeing it, I choked back tears and remembered the land I came from, the sturdiness of the people who lived on that soil, the strength of An and Herman when facing intruders to their community, their courage in protecting strangers. The rainbow, promise of hope after disaster, made me smile.

We kept driving towards Irnsum, arriving about 25 minutes late. At the close of the service, An asked me to come up and tell about finding the quilts. Although I'd prepared a half page of comments, I couldn't speak a word, still

The rainbow in the Friesland sky on that September Sunday morning, 1994.

The quilts are transferred from An's care to Lynn's.

overcome with emotion. An spoke for both of us. The quilts, packed in a wooden chest, were carried to our car by their honor guard—An and Herman's two sons. The exchange complete, the anniversary couple rode off in a carriage pulled by dapper gray horses.

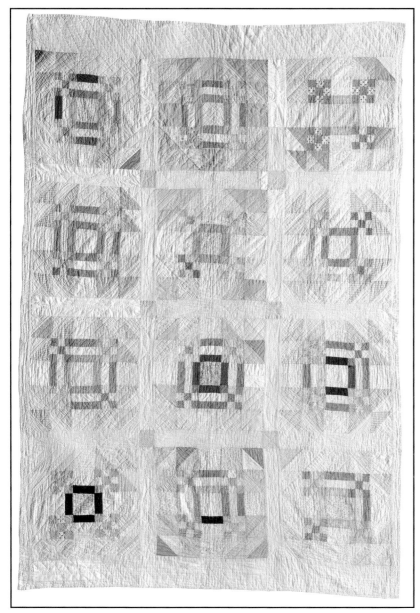

Goose in a Pond

Lynn and An

An—July 1991
In touch with my memories

For years my only contact with the War-time experiences was through those few worn quilts which were left behind after all our guests took with them whatever they needed. I sorted my memories as I folded and unfolded the quilts, telling them my unspoken tales. In those moments I allowed myself to wonder what had happened to all the souls who had sought shelter under secret Frisian roofs.

Finally in 1991, my mind was set to rest. In Winnipeg, Manitoba, Canada, on the final day of the Mennonite World Conference Assembly, a Dutch friend and I were resting in a cafeteria just outside the conference hall. Two other women sat at the same long table, and one of them kept looking at me very intensely. I didn't recognize her. After a while, she said in very slow Dutch, "In 1946 I lived in Amsterdam at a minister's house in the Vossiusstraat. Every week I had to scrub the staircase . . . "

". . . All twenty-four steps!" I finished her sentence and we laughed. The woman turned out to be Justina Neufeld, and she had found her way from Russia to Amsterdam at age 15, with her family. Taking out a Canadian Mennonite magazine with her family portrait on the cover, she pointed to the faces, one by one. "This one died on the way. This one we lost track of. This one got to Paraguay but died of typhoid fever." And so on and on. "All these losses," she said, "and no one in America understands my grief."

As I looked at her sad, sad face, I felt the unspoken grief and worry of those same years bubbling up inside me, too. I clasped her to me and we both collapsed into a 20-minute sobbing session, out of reach from the people around us. Relieved, we held each other at arm's length, looked for the first time into faces cleared by the tears of unspeakable sorrow, and laughed together. It had taken 45 years to let our feelings out.

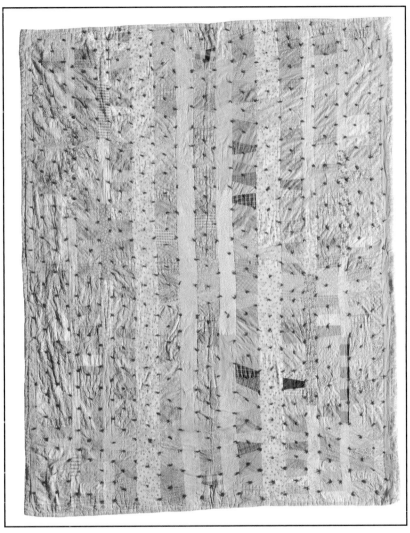

Bars and Tumblers Comforter, Number 2

Lynn
A closing word

A quilt is a blanket with a heartbeat. Next to the immaterial idea of God, is there a *material* object which better offers comfort and memories of home, and which more convincingly bears hope for those who follow us?

For hundreds of years, across large sections of the earth, women have been reworking pieces of cloth with fond memories, or cutting fresh fabric pieces and then arranging them into artistic patterns, many times women's only recognized expression of their true sentiments.

What, physically, is a quilt? Three layers of cloth are bound together to make these bed coverings. In years gone by, the bottom layer was often an old sheet of flour sack. The middle layer, also known as filling or batting, could be an old blanket, salvaged of new or used cloth, fashioned by hand or a sewing machine into a textile story. The decorative top layer featured traditional quilt patterns, often with descriptive names: Jacob's Ladder, Log Cabin, Double Wedding Ring, Drunkard's Path, and Mariner's Compass, for example. While each quiltmaker may have followed a traditional pattern, each chose her own fabric and executed the familiar pattern in her own way, so as to bring into being the story she wanted to tell.

These bed covers' three layers are bound together with knots (a comforter) or with tiny stitches (a quilt) which go through all three thicknesses. The tiny hand-stitches on a quilt are laid down in an intricate pattern over the whole face of the quilt. Sometimes this quilting (putting in the stitches) is done by groups of women who get together to do the job, and to talk, visit, and ultimately support each other while doing so.

Both quilts and comforters may be made from used clothing and/or blankets, a kind of recycling of fabrics. Less fragile, a comforter may have its filling shift as it's used; when it does, the comforter can be opened, and its filling rearranged, and then retied to extend its life.

Conceived in care, these blankets cover our physical bodies through nights of hope and wonder; they warm us after misunderstandings, comfort the sick, soften the parting of the dying. All the while they soak up the emotions which surround them and which leave an invisible yet indelible pattern in the cloth.

A quilt is hardly ever thrown away but is passed on and on from dear one to dear one. Or, if needed elsewhere, it is given to a stranger across the world who has no other blanket. Such were the MCC quilts conserved by An Keuning-Tichelaar. Refugees renewed their strength under these quilts, then traveled on to South or North America in search of a new and safe home. As she sorted her memories of those turbulent years, An unfolded and then refolded the quilts that were left behind, imbuing them with tales unspoken. And she wondered what happened to all the souls whom she had helped to find shelter under secret Frisian roofs.

These particular quilts drew An and me together. We met, we talked, she wrote. I realized the power of her stories and wanted her to share them, but she was circumspect at first. I had the quilts restored and exhibited, and as I observed their effect on viewers, and the impact of An's accompanying stories, I realized that I must find a way to get both out into the world.

The contrasts between our lives helped drive An and me to complete this project. She stayed put, rooted in the history of her family and in service to her chosen church. I was, like my forebears, on the move. Surprisingly, I ended up back where they started from several hundred years previous. An struggled with confining roles and expectations; I struggled to make a family in three cultures and abandoned hope of living up to the expectations of any group. I'm marginal and have been shaped by the world, yet the quilts have connected me to my new home. Firmly established in her home area, the quilts have given An wings and a chance to prove, even at 82 years of age, that her stories merit being written and that others are interested in them.

For three years, these quilts, which now seem to belong to all of us, will travel across North America to many of the communities where they were made. Then they will return to Europe to tell their story about the gracious women who made them and gave them to comfort strangers, of the strong men and women who risked their own comfort for principle, of the refugees who received solace from strangers. Finally, the quilts will be given a permanent home in a proposed meeting place near Witmarsum, Friesland, to be known as the International Menno Simons Center Netherlands.

My wish is that the communities who made these quilts, and then saw that others were able to use them in their time of desperate need, will understand in a deeper way the value of the help they gave in the War years. I also hope that these work-weary quilts will inspire all of us to help, in whatever small or common way we can, when a need is before us, even when—*especially* when—we feel inadequate to the task.

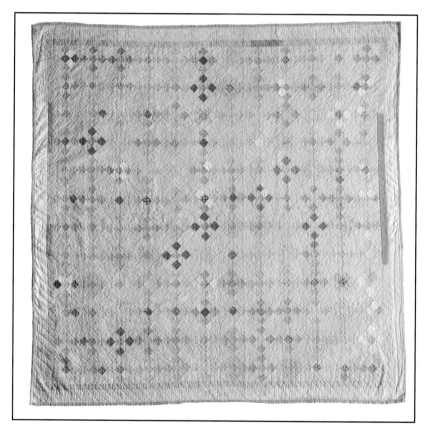

Scrap Nine-Patch

About the Quilts

Bars and Tumblers Comforter, Number 1 (opposite title page), 89 x 72

This comforter mirrors the traditional Bars design. Moving out from the center, the lengthwise bars are made up of tumbler shapes, then squares and rectangles. The individual pieces were cut freehand. The cover is knotted, not quilted.

Bars and Tumblers Comforter Number 2 (page 176), 90 x 70

This scrappy comforter, and its sister comforter of a similar design (opposite the title page), share many of the same fabrics.

This one's vertical bars are generally more defined. Many of the tumblers making up those bars are smaller in this cover. Displaying an intense frugality, the maker(s) pieced scraps in order to complete the bars.

Because of the overlap in technique and fabrics, it is likely that both Bars and Tumblers comforters were made by the same sewing circle.

Bow Ties (page 167), 79 x 70

This scrappy quilt is loosely arranged, with many of the darker colors running up and down, and the lighter colors going from side to side.

A clam-shell quilting design is spread across the quilt, executed with varying levels of skill.

Crazy Stars and Dresden Plates (page 156), 74¾ x 59

Puckered from washing, wear, and fabrics of varying stretch and durability, this comforter retains some of its original warmth and glow.

Six stars, each made of eight diamonds, which are composed of multiple fabrics cut crazy-patch style, share the face of the quilt with six Dresden plates, each made of 13 spokes, each of a single fabric. Consequently, the stars dominate, additionally because they're of brighter fabrics than the stars.

Between the stars, and at the center of each plate, is one fabric, a busy neutral of black triangles and dots on a beige field.

Dresden Plate (page 127), 86 x 72

Despite hard use, the appliqued patches have held strong, suggesting that one woman did the appliqueing. In contrast, the quilting appears to have been a group effort since the distances between the "plates" and the quilting surrounding them vary considerably.

The border is not as faded as the center of the quilt, perhaps indicating that the border fell over the edge of the bed where it was less subject to direct use and sunlight.

Strips of floral fabric were used alternately in the outer rows of piecing that define the side borders.

Double Four-Patch with Diagonal Squares (page 144), 89 x 62

Although the quiltmaker followed a basic design, she was not restricted by it. She created strong diagonal motion across much of the face of this quilt, even though the fabrics used to make individual paths aren't exactly alike the whole way across the quilt. Micro-dot or shirting fabric was paired with more richly colored fabric to gain this diagonal effect.

The sizes of each square, as well as the size and amount of quilting stitches, indicate that this was made with the care and precision typical of a quilt to be given to a family member.

The fabric is threadbare and the batting shows through in many places. The larger squares in the double four-patches are made of stronger fabrics which have survived better than many of the smaller squares.

Dutchman's Puzzle (page 12), 88 x 61

This quilt is more carefully designed than many quilts made for "relief." The pieced patches are composed entirely of triangles; all of the fabrics are plain rather than prints.

Perhaps the quilt was made for a family member, given its pleasing scale, its predictable execution, its delicate binding. The quilting itself is utilitarian, done mostly in straight lines with comparatively large stitches.

Goose in the Pond (page 173), 90 x 60

Despite fading, the piecing consistency of this quilt can still be seen, or imagined: off-white center squares are edged by black bars, each with corner blocks. Those corner blocks also belong to a nine-patch block which composes part of the next ring of piecing.

There is both consistency and surprise here. The large pieced blocks include quite a variety of contrasting fabrics. Cream sashing and borders surround those blocks, punctuated by six blue or mauve squares that sit at intersections in the central part of the quilt.

Hole in the Barn Door (page 128), 70 x 59

As is typical of many quilts made for daily use, this one has a predictable pattern with obvious deviations!

Perhaps this quilt was suddenly needed. Note that only two rows of blocks, and only half the large center squares, are quilted, apart from some stitches that were put in randomly elsewhere.

Log Cabin (page 9), 87 x 71

Might this quilt be a remnant of a larger quilt, since the overall Barn-Raising arrangement of the patches appears to have been disrupted? Four newer patches were added to the top of the quilt at some point—made with brighter colors and better workmanship than on the rest of the quilt. The fabrics throughout have a somewhat Victorian character.

Monkey Wrench (page 136), 78 x 57

This scrap quilt uses only three shapes—squares, triangles, and rectangles. Depending upon the combination of fabrics, some of the pieced patches create the illusion of being octagons.

The quilt appears to have been done in a hurry, or it may have been the work of a beginner. The large unpieced blocks have a minimum amount of quilting stitches.

Nine-Patch (denim) (page 93), 78 x 54

The small squares in the nine-patch blocks are of varying blue fabrics; the micro-dot fabric is consistent throughout.

The use of denim implies that the quilt was prepared for hard wear. Despite that, the quilting stitches are abundant and fine. Cable patterns, with diamonds between the loops, fill the light inner borders.

Rectangle (page 141), 75 x 66

This quilting showcase is an ever-enlarging set of rectangles, made of sizeable stretches of fabric, instead of small pieces from a scrapbag.

A graceful quilted medallion fills the center area. (Notice how it is framed with quilting stitches in each corner of that light central block.) Lovely cable quilting in the inner light borders converges in each corner into a floral shape with cross-hatching. (Note the unusual diagonal seams in each corner of this inner border.) Diagonal quilting fills the colored areas. (Observe how the quilting lines switch direction in the corners of the outer colored border.)

Scrap Nine-Patch (page 1799), 78 x 78

Although a scrappy quilt, this cover gives a few clues that it may have been a "family" quilt. A floral quilting pattern fills the larger plain blocks, situated between the nine-patch blocks. In addition, most of the nine-patch blocks have some shade of red as their center square, creating a focal point for each pieced block.

The nine-patch blocks, and their plain-block counterparts, all stand on point, giving delicate drama to this quilt, made quieter by fading from washing and, perhaps, sunlight.

Shoo-Fly (page 169), 86 x 62

The pieced patches in this carefully planned quilt are made of triangles and squares. Salmon-colored squares in the alternating horizontal rows of pieced blocks, and the salmon borders, bring a visual unity to the top.

Attempts to repair the quilt—and a wide variety of original fabrics—have not undone the quilt's unmistakable design.

Stars and Chinese Coins (page 121), 86 x 80

This exuberant comforter is likely the work of a beginner. An "organically" shaped hexagon is at the center of each star. A Chinese-coin piecing effect borders each star and is echoed in the top and bottom inner borders.

The edges of the stars were sacrificed along the sides of the comforter, perhaps to make it a particular size.

The fabrics are unlikely to have been left from clothing projects. Multi-colored yarn knots hold the layers together, rather than quilt stitches.

Stars and Triangles (page 151), 87 x 49

Here are pinwheels (each made of eight equilateral triangles) at the center of stars (each composed of 16 elongated triangles). Set between these stars are squares that are each composed of four equilateral triangles. The effect is an alive quilt, reinforced by the use of bright, unrestful fabrics.

The quilt is well constructed. There is little puckering. Most of the points are sharp and meet the points of the adjoining pieces.

Four orange plaid and purple patches are set systematically into the quilt, and yet they bring a chaotic burst of energy to the whole piece.

String Stars (page 161), 76 x 58

This quilt's carnival atmosphere stands in contrast to the sober, predictable fabrics and arrangements customarily made by Mennonite families and sewing circles of this period and earlier.

The piecing is messy and there is no quilting, yet the stars are of nearly equal color tones; the plain blue blocks and borders are not dominated by the pieced patches. The little squares set on point between the stars add to the visual drama.

Triangles and Hexagons (page 33), 73 x 63

In this highly geometric quilt, triangles are combined in groups of three brightly colored fabrics and three more neutral shades to create hexagons.

The piecing required much planning, as did the dramatic and precisely bound side edges.

The quilting stitches are small and consistent and appear ⅛" inside the seams. The design, piecing, and quilting were likely the work of one person.

Zigzag (page 154), 88 x 66

Composed entirely of triangles, this quilt is dramatically effective because of the way in which the colors are used together—and in juxtaposition to each other. Additionally, quilting appears on only one side of the triangles, reinforcing the zigzag pattern.

The quilting stitches are of many lengths; apparently the cover was quilted by a group.

Mennonite Relief Efforts Today

Mennonite Central Committee (MCC) is a relief, service, and peace agency of the North American Mennonite and Brethren in Christ churches.

MCC held its first official meeting on September 27, 1920. MCC's name is a reflection of this coming together of different church groups into one "central" committee. The MCC mission statement reflects the biblical call to care for the hungry and the thirsty, the stranger and the naked, the sick and those in prison (Matthew 25:35-36). The goal of peacemaking is the well-being of all people.

For more information, see www.mcc.org.

The present Dutch Mennonite relief organization is the Foundation for Special Needs (*Bijzondere Noden*), nicknamed "BN." Its roots are in the General Commission for Foreign Needs founded in 1695. In 1982, the focus was changed from "foreign needs" only to "special plights, domestic as well as foreign." BN works as a partner with local church communities as well as other Mennonite institutions, both Dutch and non-Dutch, to relieve need.

Further, BN is a close partner with the German Mennonite relief agencies. Together they form an umbrella organization, named IMO, which supports projects in 12 countries. MCC is a valued sister organization.

There is hardly a group of Mennonites on the globe whose founding seeds were not directly or indirectly nurtured by the Dutch Mennonites through their relief organizations. Although they who were givers became receivers for a short period in the mid-20th century, within a very short time they were again sending help to other Mennonite groups in greater need.

If you want to give a quilt or comforter to "relief," and would like to make one yourself, there are simple patterns in the book, *Quick Colorful Quilts*, available on the Good Books secure website, www.goodbks.com.

If you want to help a child make a quilt or comforter for "relief," there are simple patterns in *The Boy and the Quilt*. This book is also available at www.goodbks.com.

About Makkum Pottery

Royal Tichelaar Makkum earthenware and tiles are prized by museums and individuals over the world by virtue of their colorful beauty, variety of design, and traditional handcraftsmanship. Each piece is still made by hand in the factory at Makkum, using a technique called majolica. By painting the ornamentation directly onto the raw tin glaze, brilliant colors can be captured in the firing. Royal Tichelaar Makkum remains faithful to this technique which brought considerable fame to the Netherlands in the 17th and 18th centuries.

While other Dutch earthenware producers have adopted more modern techniques, the Tichelaar family decided to keep the technique but expand to include experimental modern designs. Their tile selection is considerable, with seven colors of white alone. Almost nothing is impossible for them to make, including ridge tiles for thatched roofs and artist's commissions.

The clay used is gotten from a nearby hamlet and enriched with lime. A piece of Makkum pottery is literally a piece of Friesland. Every Mennonite church in the Netherlands has had a Makkum plate with traditional blue design and the same words, which remind the viewer that deeds are preferable to words (see the statement at the bottom of page 163).

The Proposed International Menno Simons Center Netherlands

The Mennonite Church Council in the Netherlands (ADS) is planning to build a fitting meeting place and visitors' center close to an existing monument, which commemorates Menno Simons' life and work, near Witmarsum. The monument also marks the place where one of the oldest Mennonite churches in the region stood. This is where Menno Simons joined the Anabaptists, later becoming one of their well-known leaders.

The International Menno Simons Center Netherlands (IMSCN) is designed to be a location where people can receive information about and inspiration from a spiritual past, a place where there is room to deeply consider social and spiritual matters. The goal is:

- to develop, build, and maintain a meeting place for Mennonites and other related faith communities;
- to make the facilities available to persons interested in freedom of speech and belief and related cultural and historical topics, so that they may deepen, enrich, and expand their understanding;
- to develop new perspectives on freedom of speech and belief, together and alone.

Initial plans were presented on September 11, 2004, the 125th anniversary of the monument. Together with diverse partners from Europe, the Americas, and hopefully other continents, the overseeing group hopes to refine the plans, build support, and begin to gather funds in 2005. Within a few years, the center hopes to welcome Mennonites from all over the world, on historic ground, with the MCC quilts from An Keuning hanging on the walls.

The authors of *Passing On the Comfort: The War, the Quilts, and the Women Who Made a Difference* are donating their royalties to the realization of this, or a similar, project.

Readings and Sources

Bergen, Mary. [2001]. *Journey to Freedom: The Story of Jakob and Maria Redekop.* N.p.

Dyck, Peter & Elfrieda. 1991. *Up From the Rubble.* Scottdale, PA: Herald Press.

Friesen, Edith Elisabeth. 2003. *Journey into Freedom.* Winnipeg, MB: Raduga Publications.

Gibbons, Phoebe Earle. 2001. *Pennsylvania Dutch & Other Essays.* Mechanicsburg, PA: Stackpole Books.

Hoover, Paul S. 1998. *In the Name of Christ: The Beginnings of the Pennsylvania MCC Relief Sale.* Akron, PA: Mennonite Central Committee.

Horst, Hans van der. 2001. *The Low Sky: Understanding the Dutch.* Schiedam, The Netherlands: Scriptum.

Horst, Irvin B. 1950. *A Ministry of Goodwill: A Short Account of Mennonite Relief 1939-1949.* Akron, PA: Mennonite Central Committee. Page 15.

Jong, Louis de. 1956. *The German Fifth Column in the Second World War.* Chicago, IL: University of Chicago Press.

Kreider, Robert. 1988. *Interviews with Peter J. Dyck and Elfrieda Klassen Dyck.* Akron, PA: Mennonite Central Committee. Pages 69-125.

Roegholt, Dr. Richter. 2004. *A Short History of Amsterdam.* Amersfoort, The Netherlands: Bekking & Blitz.

Rubin, Susan Goldman. 2003. *Searching for Anne Frank: Letters from Amsterdam to Iowa.* New York, NY: Harry N. Abrams, Inc.

Ruth, John Landis. 2001. *The Earth Is the Lord's: A Narrative History of the Lancaster Mennonite Conference.* Scottdale, PA: Herald Press.

Schroeder, William. 1990. *Mennonite Historical Atlas.* Winnipeg, MB: Springfield Publishers.

Tobin, Jacqueline L. and Raymond G. Dobard, Ph.D. 1999. *Hidden in Plain View: A Secret Story of Quilts and the Underground Railroad.* New York, NY: Doubleday.

Voth, Norma Jost. 1990. *Mennonite Foods & Folkways from South Russia, Vol. 1.* Intercourse, PA: Good Books.